Making Design Theory

Design Thinking, Design Theory

Ken Friedman and Erik Stolterman, editors

Making Design Theory

Johan Redström

The MIT Press
Cambridge, Massachusetts
London, England

This book was set in ITC Stone Sans Std and ITC Stone Serif Std by Toppan Best-set Premedia Limited. Printed and bound in the United States of America.

Library of Congress Cataloging-in-Publication Data

Names: Redström, Johan, author.
Title: Making design theory / Johan Redström.
Description: Cambridge, MA : The MIT Press, 2017. | Series: Design thinking, design theory | Includes bibliographical references and index.
Identifiers: LCCN 2016059703 | ISBN 9780262036658 (hardcover : alk. paper)
Subjects: LCSH: Design--Philosophy.
Classification: LCC NK1505 .R43 2017 | DDC 745.401--dc23 LC record available at https://lccn.loc.gov/2016059703

10   9   8   7   6   5   4   3   2   1

For Arvid, Ivar, Alve, and Maria

Contents

Series Foreword

As professions go, design is relatively young. The practice of design predates professions. In fact, the practice of design—making things to serve a useful goal, making tools—predates the human race. Making tools is one of the attributes that made us human in the first place.

Design, in the most generic sense of the word, began over 2.5 million years ago when *Homo habilis* manufactured the first tools. Human beings were designing well before we began to walk upright. Four hundred thousand years ago, we began to manufacture spears. By forty thousand years ago, we had moved up to specialized tools.

Urban design and architecture came along ten thousand years ago in Mesopotamia. Interior architecture and furniture design probably emerged with them. It was another five thousand years before graphic design and typography got their start in Sumeria with the development of cuneiform. After that, things picked up speed.

All goods and services are designed. The urge to design—to consider a situation, imagine a better situation, and act to create that improved situation—goes back to our prehuman ancestors. Making tools helped us to become what we are—design helped to make us human.

Today, the word "design" means many things. The common factor linking them is service, and designers are engaged in a service profession in which the results of their work meet human needs.

Design is first of all a process. The word "design" entered the English language in the 1500s as a verb, with the first written citation of the verb dated to the year 1548. *Merriam-Webster's Collegiate Dictionary* defines the verb "design" as "to conceive and plan out in the mind; to have as a specific purpose; to devise for a specific function or end." Related to these is the act of drawing, with an emphasis on the nature of the drawing as a plan or map, as well as "to draw plans for; to create, fashion, execute or construct according to plan."

Half a century later, the word began to be used as a noun, with the first cited use of the noun "design" occurring in 1588. *Merriam-Webster's* defines the noun as "a particular purpose held in view by an individual or group; deliberate, purposive planning; a mental project or scheme in which means to an end are laid down." Here, too, purpose and planning toward desired outcomes are central. Among these are "a preliminary sketch or outline showing the main features of something to be executed; an underlying scheme that governs functioning, developing or unfolding; a plan or protocol for carrying out or accomplishing something; the arrangement of elements or details in a product or work of art." Today, we design large, complex process, systems, and services, and we design organizations and structures to produce them. Design has changed considerably since our remote ancestors made the first stone tools.

At a highly abstract level, Herbert Simon's definition covers nearly all imaginable instances of design. To design, Simon writes, is to "[devise] courses of action aimed at changing existing situations into preferred ones" (Simon, *The Sciences of the Artificial*, 2nd ed., MIT Press, 1982, p. 129). Design, properly defined, is the entire process across the full range of domains required for any given outcome.

But the design process is always more than a general, abstract way of working. Design takes concrete form in the work of the service professions that meet human needs, a broad range of making and planning disciplines. These include industrial design, graphic design, textile design, furniture design, information design, process design, product design, interaction design, transportation design, educational design, systems design, urban design, design leadership, and design management, as well as architecture, engineering, information technology, and computer science.

These fields focus on different subjects and objects. They have distinct traditions, methods, and vocabularies, used and put into practice by distinct and often dissimilar professional groups. Although the traditions dividing these groups are distinct, common boundaries sometimes form a border. Where this happens, they serve as meeting points where common concerns build bridges. Today, ten challenges uniting the design professions form such a set of common concerns.

Three performance challenges, four substantive challenges, and three contextual challenges bind the design disciplines and professions together as a common field. The performance challenges arise because all design professions:

1. act on the physical world;
2. address human needs; and
3. generate the built environment.

In the past, these common attributes were not sufficient to transcend the boundaries of tradition. Today, objective changes in the larger world give rise to four substantive challenges that are driving convergence in design practice and research. These substantive challenges are:

1. increasingly ambiguous boundaries between artifacts, structure, and process;
2. increasingly large-scale social, economic, and industrial frames;
3. an increasingly complex environment of needs, requirements, and constraints; and
4. information content that often exceeds the value of physical substance.

These challenges require new frameworks of theory and research to address contemporary problem areas while solving specific cases and problems. In professional design practice, we often find that solving design problems requires interdisciplinary teams with a transdisciplinary focus. Fifty years ago, a sole practitioner and an assistant or two might have solved most design problems; today, we need groups of people with skills across several disciplines, and the additional skills that enable professionals to work with, listen to, and learn from each other as they solve problems.

Three contextual challenges define the nature of many design problems today. While many design problems function at a simpler level, these issues affect many of the major design problems that challenge us, and these challenges also affect simple design problems linked to complex social, mechanical, or technical systems. These issues are:

1. a complex environment in which many projects or products cross the boundaries of several organizations, stakeholder, producer, and user groups;
2. projects or products that must meet the expectations of many organizations, stakeholders, producers, and users; and

3. demands at every level of production, distribution, reception, and control.

These ten challenges require a qualitatively different approach to professional design practice than was the case in earlier times. Past environments were simpler. They made simpler demands. Individual experience and personal development were sufficient for depth and substance in professional practice. While experience and development are still necessary, they are no longer sufficient. Most of today's design challenges require analytic and synthetic planning skills that cannot be developed through practice alone.

Professional design practice today involves advanced knowledge. This knowledge is not solely a higher level of professional practice. It is also a qualitatively different form of professional practice that emerges in response to the demands of the information society and the knowledge economy to which it gives rise.

In a recent essay ("Why Design Education Must Change," *Core77*, November 26, 2010), Donald Norman challenges the premises and practices of the design profession. In the past, designers operated on the belief that talent and a willingness to jump into problems with both feet gives them an edge in solving problems. Norman writes:

In the early days of industrial design, the work was primarily focused upon physical products. Today, however, designers work on organizational structure and social problems, on interaction, service, and experience design. Many problems involve complex social and political issues. As a result, designers have become applied behavioral scientists, but they are woefully undereducated for the task. Designers often fail to understand the complexity of the issues and the depth of knowledge already known. They claim that fresh eyes can produce novel solutions, but then they wonder why these solutions are seldom implemented, or if implemented, why they fail. Fresh eyes can indeed produce insightful results, but the eyes must also be educated and knowledgeable. Designers often lack the requisite understanding. Design schools do not train students about these complex issues, about the interlocking complexities of human and social behavior, about the behavioral sciences, technology, and business. There is little or no training in science, the scientific method, and experimental design.

This is not industrial design in the sense of designing products, but industry-related design, design as thought and action for solving problems and imagining new futures. This new MIT Press series of books emphasizes strategic design to create value through innovative products and services, and it emphasizes design as service through rigorous creativity, critical inquiry, and an ethics of respectful design. This rests on a sense of understanding, empathy, and appreciation for people, for nature, and for the world we shape through design. Our goal as editors is to develop a series of vital conversations that help designers and researchers to serve business, industry, and the public sector for positive social and economic outcomes.

We will present books that bring a new sense of inquiry to the design, helping to shape a more reflective and stable design discipline able to support a stronger profession grounded in empirical research, generative concepts, and the solid theory that gives rise to what W. Edwards Deming described as profound knowledge (Deming, *The New Economics for Industry, Government, Education*, MIT, Center for Advanced Engineering Study, 1993). For Deming, a physicist, engineer, and designer, profound knowledge comprised systems thinking and the understanding of processes embedded in systems; an understanding of variation and the tools we need to understand variation; a theory of knowledge; and a foundation in human psychology. This is the beginning of "deep design"—the union of deep practice with robust intellectual inquiry.

A series on design thinking and theory faces the same challenges that we face as a profession. On one level, design is a general human process that we use to understand and to shape our world. Nevertheless, we cannot address this process or the world in its general, abstract form. Rather, we meet the challenges of design in specific challenges, addressing problems or ideas in a situated context. The challenges we face as designers today are as diverse as the problems clients bring us. We are involved in design for economic anchors, economic continuity, and economic growth. We design for urban needs and rural needs, for social development and creative communities. We are involved with environmental sustainability and economic policy, agriculture competitive crafts for export, competitive products and brands for micro-enterprises, developing new products for bottom-of-pyramid markets and redeveloping old products for mature or wealthy markets. Within the framework of design, we are also challenged to design for extreme situations, for biotech, nanotech, and new materials, and design for social business, as well as conceptual challenges for worlds that do not yet exist such as the world beyond the Kurzweil singularity—and for new visions of the world that does exist.

The Design Thinking, Design Theory series from the MIT Press will explore these issues and more—meeting them, examining them, and helping designers to address them.

Join us in this journey.

Ken Friedman   Erik Stolterman
Editors, Design Thinking, Design Theory Series

Acknowledgments

Given the inherently collaborative character of both design and research, it is a somewhat strange thing to write a book about it on your own. Indeed, appearances can be deceiving, and this book would certainly not exist without the collaborations, dialogues, discussions, and debates that I have had the pleasure to participate in. In particular, my deepest gratitude for years of exciting conversations, critical feedback, and important ideas to Thomas Binder, Carl DiSalvo, Pelle Ehn, Peter Gall Krogh, Maria Göransdotter, Lars Hallnäs, Jamer Hunt, Kia Höök, Ilpo Koskinen, Monica Lindh Karlsson, Jonas Löwgren, Ramia Mazé, Maria Redström, Erik Stolterman, Heather Wiltse, and Christina Zetterlund. Special thanks also to all PhD students I have had the pleasure to work with, in particular during recent years here at Umeå Institute of Design: Lorenzo Davoli, Guido Hermans, Aditya Pawar, Stoffel Kuenen, Tara Mullaney, Søren Rosenbak, Daniela Rothkegel, and Ru Zarin. Thanks to the staff and students at Umeå Institute of Design, Umeå University, for making this such an outstanding place to work.

Many thanks to Umeå University for additional research funding, and to Baltic for funding the "Prototyping Practice" research program. Special thanks to Marije de Haas for greatly improving the illustrations, to the series editors Ken Friedman and Erik Stolterman, and to Douglas Sery and Susan Buckley of MIT Press for making this book possible.

To family and friends, mom and dad, Maria, Arvid, Ivar and Alve: thanks for everything.

1 Thing and Theory

This book is about theory development in design research driven by practice, experimentation, and making. It is not about theorizing practice, or looking into design from the outside and aiming to articulate its general structures. Rather, it is about exploring the idea that as design research engages in making many different kinds of things, theory might well be one of those things it is—or could be—making. And so the question is, what design theory could be made in research through design?

It is not hard to find enough potential contradictions to disregard such questions, leaving them to prevalent disciplinary distribution of tasks where makers make and theorists theorize, as if the two were completely separate matters of concern. Yet with the accumulation of design research deeply committed to practices of making and the increasing presence of more conceptual and discursive approaches to design, there comes a need to yet again ask whether previous perspectives on theory and practice still hold, or if other possibilities are now emerging as the result of new forms of design and research.

At times it seems as if one of the key characteristics of design is to base its very existence on the complexities arising from dichotomies. To negotiate form *and* function. To be about craft and skill *and* work with industrial production. To link production *and* consumption. To work with free and open processes *and* to be deeply committed to method. To be user centered *and* design driven. To be art *and* science. Sometimes the intellectual instability of being in the middle is so overwhelming that we are tempted to give in to the at least academically much more convenient positions on either side: to choose between theory *or* practice, art *or* science, and so on. But design can also be remarkably resilient and willing to commit to all that which is neither black nor white, but complex and colorful.

Indeed, design's capacity to deal with complexity and conflicting concerns is perhaps its most fascinating feature. What follows stems from an idea that this ability to address complexity is inherently intertwined with design's resilience to reductive dichotomies. More specifically, it comes out of a hunch that a key reason we enjoy dichotomies so much in design is because they allow us to address conflict, collision, and contradiction, opening up new perspectives and potentials as a result. As is the case here: to ask the question of what design theory is *made* in the context of practice-based design research is to ask for trouble. And trouble is precisely what we want.

Thus this inquiry may appear as taking a contradiction of terms as its starting point: with notions of theory as that which is abstracted from, generalized over, and said about something, would not design be its object rather than the method of its making? And so this issue is my target here: to look into the character of design theory using the articulation of a new kind as the method. This will of course not yield a general answer to what design theory is, but perhaps it might offer an alternative example of what it could be. I will call it "transitional theory," a kind of design theory that is inherently unstable, fluid, and dynamic in character. And keeping to one of the basic ideas of research through design, it is through the making of this new transitional theory—the making of this *example*—that we might learn something, hopefully also about design theory per se.

The overall purpose of this book is to propose an alternative approach to theory development in the context of design research driven by practice, by experimentation and making. My ambition is not to prove this approach to be right but rather to open up something akin to a design space for theory development within design research. My approach is to try to shift perspectives—if only slightly—to provide short glimpses of something else. Thus much of what I present here builds on ways of breaking things apart, of unpacking positions and statements that are so familiar we perhaps do not see their potential.

The basic idea is to create this shift in perspective by evoking the temporality of theory: by considering theory as something not always stable and constant, but in this case as something unfolding, something acted as much as articulated, performed as much as described. There is a relevant etymological relation between "theory" and "tourism": in its original meaning, the Greek word *theoria* meant to see something, to be a spectator, or "in its most literal sense, 'witnessing a spectacle'" (Nightingale 2001, 23). Perhaps the approach taken here can be seen in the light of this early history of philosophy: "theory" approached as something meant to take you places so as to witness a spectacle.

Many important aspects of what design and design research are about will not be addressed here, and I make no claim to account for what design, design research, or design theory *in general* are. For instance, I will not discuss what it is that a designer does when designing, how practices of designing unfold, or how design research is practically set up and conducted in a given situation. Given that this book is about practice and research through design, this approach may seem odd. Making, however, happens on many levels, and to expose what I would like to discuss here, it is necessary to turn to, and focus on, the conceptual structures seemingly coming to expression in and through designing. As I will try to show, matters related what is typically considered as theoretical, such as definitions of central terms and concepts, are also sometimes literally made by hand.

This means that I will try to stay away from many of the complexities stemming from the assemblages of people, materials, funding, institutional contexts, and a range of other matters that tie poetics and politics together in design. Of course, the ways that these sociomaterial assemblages are formed and performed also define the work that unfolds, what is possible and what is not. My somewhat isolated focus on abstract aspects of theory making in research through design does not stem from an idea that this research is somehow free from all this, objective in its approach, neutral in its outcome. On the contrary, my reason for discussing some of these conceptual structures is that they bring something to these assemblages, and only by first calling them to the foreground will we be able to more clearly see this. In other words, my goal is to add something to our understanding of design research by unpacking some—but not all—of its structures.

Explain Yourself!

With the growing community of design researchers working with formats based on experimentation and practice, there also comes a more extensive discourse on this kind of research (cf. Joost et al. 2016; Koskinen et al. 2011). Still, within the larger frameworks of academia and its funding structures, much of this research still faces significant challenges when arguing not only for its merit but also for its method in the context of more established modes of inquiry. Further, research through design is by no means a homogeneous category, and it is important to acknowledge that a significant variety is present. At the same time, there are also shared concerns and a number of foundational issues that many of us struggle with. And so when I, for instance, discuss my own work as if it was typical, I do so in the sense of offering examples, not exemplars. They are illustrations of practice, not "best practice," and I use them because they allow me to tell the stories of how I came into contact and worked with these issues.

The reason I work with my own material is that this inquiry begins with the feeling of having to explain oneself—and thus importantly also the issue of not being able to fully do just that. As designers and researchers, we are responsible not only for the results of our work but very much also for the point from which we start: the perspectives and positions, as well as the presence of certain privileges, that are often as implicit as they are fundamental conditions for our work. But being accountable does not necessarily mean that we can fully account for our point of departure, as only parts of what we take for granted are clearly visible to us. This is just one reason we depend on the perspectives and critiques of others to also understand ourselves.

Indeed, the importance of *difference* when it comes to both definitions and perspectives in design is one of the main ideas throughout this book, and it is crucial to read this text in light of the inevitable limitations of its partial perspectives and particular circumstances. This is why it needs to begin with the task of explaining oneself, not with some panoptical ambition to instruct others.

Defining Design

If we take theories to, in general, be things that in one way or another describe and explain something, that reveal and articulate the underlying structures, principles, or logic of something, then we also have to remember that we do not have just a theory but always a theory *of* something. Theories have a direction, an orientation, a purpose—and this purpose determines what needs to be accounted for and what can be considered the matter of something else. This means that there might be a significant difference between a theory *of* design and a *design* theory of something. If a theory *of* design would take design as its subject, with the aim of developing an account of its underlying structures and logic as seen from the outside, what would a *design* theory of something be like?

In what follows, I explore this question on the basis of two initial ideas: first, that the notion of *design* theory (as potentially different from theory *of* design) calls for an inquiry into how theory is made in and through (rather than about) design and designing; and second, that we might therefore have to consider certain conceptual elements and structures produced and performed in research through design as theoretical, even though they do not look like the kinds of theory we are familiar with from other domains.

Moreover, design theory in this sense will also be *about* something; it will be design theory *of* something. To stay at a very basic level, I try to address this directedness by focusing on terms and concepts that we use to articulate this "of." One of the most important ways that we ground the direction of a theory is by using definitions, how we define the basic terms that we use to articulate what something is all about.

With respect to the importance of definitions for setting directions, the very notion of design theory implies a complicated starting point, as we lack an agreed-on and unified definition of what design is in the first place. Earlier I talked about design as if we all know what it is. I have talked about design as if *it* had certain capabilities and properties, as if we agreed that there is something distinct we can call design and that has such characteristics. As if we agree on what the term "design" actually refers to, and we already share this basic understanding and definition. This is certainly not the case. More likely, what has happened so far is that you have begun to form an idea of what part of the pool of perspectives on design I might be swimming in. Terms such as "research through design" perhaps made you think about certain kinds of research efforts, and with an overall orientation seemingly pointing to notions of design as in "*design* schools," you begin to form an idea about what kind of "design" we are talking about here. Then you might try to place this initial positioning of my use of "design" in relation to other such notions you have encountered, placing me somewhere on a map that most likely spans many more such positions and perspectives.

From the perspective of basic definitions, this seems inherently problematic, as we seem to lack a solid framing of what it is that we actually talk about. Learning from other areas of research, the obvious response would therefore be to start out with providing such a definition to resolve this uncertainty. As I try to show in the coming chapters, however, I believe that the absence of one basic definition is significant, and it tells us something crucial about what is at stake in design theory. Indeed, I argue that the presence of many *different* definitions is instrumental as we try to understand and articulate what things like "design" or "designing" are; this absence of unified definitions is not a conceptual shortcoming of our thinking but in fact an effective strategy for coping with certain kinds of complexity— although this is not something we have made explicit. And so instead of starting off by providing definitions, I will begin with a set of questions regarding how definitions are made in design: If we are going to do "design theory" in research through design, how do our definitions come about? Where can we find them? How are they made? How do they function? How do they come to expression?

Overview

In this book, I sketch a picture of what design theory is made in design research, and what this making is like. This picture centers on a presentation and discussion of three different ways in which theoretical parts and structures, such as basic definitions, are made through design. The first deals with how we seem to use combinations (or spectra) of fluid terms to articulate issues and ideas in ways that discrete terms with individual meanings cannot, and what this means for how we conceive of conceptual precision in design theory (chap. 3). The second deals with how also more complex concepts can be defined through acts of making, and what this implies for how we think about the ways that different kinds of definitions may or may not support conceptual development (chap. 4). The third deals with how issues pertaining to what designing is and could be—such as its basic beliefs and worldviews—can be understood on the basis of a kind of composite definition called "programs" (chap. 5). These three different kinds of definitions made through design are building blocks we use to create conceptual structures to support design—structures that allow us to orient our efforts, describe our intentions, frame our results, and so on—and I argue that they therefore need to be considered "theoretical." I call these structures "transitional theory": something to be considered "theoretical" because of what they do and how they do this, but unlike most theories at the same time something fluid, unstable, and transitional.

I begin my discussion by looking at the critique of "weak" connections to theory in design research, and how such matters have been addressed. The focus is on articulating and analyzing three main existing tactics for resolving relations to theory, referred to as "parallels," "sequencing," and "intermediaries." Chapter 2, "Tactics," ends with a presentation of an issue that runs like a red thread throughout the text: the tension between the universal and the particular.

Chapter 3, "Between," sets out to provide a first idea of what the design space for transitional theory might be like. Tracing a trajectory through this space using the question of what it means to fundamentally redefine something in design, it paints a picture of a spectrum of definitions between products and paradigms, ranging from being about what *a* design is to what design*ing* is. The chapter ends with a discussion of what kind of precision the definitions presented can be considered to have, and what this means for how we think about theoretical precision in design theory.

Since the definitions addressed in chapter 3 can be considered very basic, chapter 4, "Making Definitions," takes the idea of making a definition through design to the realm of more complex concepts. Building the story around two examples—"form" and "user"—the chapter discusses the implications of keeping definitions stable and static. In particular, I aim to address issues related to concepts not being able to support development and what that means for how we might need to rethink how foundational concepts are defined. As a response to such issues, I discuss alternative ways of defining concepts such as form and user that instead aim for the unstable and transitional. At a more general level, these alternative definitions are meant to exemplify what making a definition through design of more complex concepts could be like, and in what ways they can be either stable and static or unstable and transitional, thus achieving precision in quite different ways.

Chapter 5, "Programs," addresses the matter of defining more complex concepts in a different direction. Whereas my discussions about form and use center on the need to open up established notions, this chapter looks at how sets of definitions made through design are combined to form structures that address matters such as worldviews or basic orientations. Here I take an in-depth look at the notion of "program," the term located at the center of the spectrum outlined in chapter 3. I do so for two main reasons: first, because of its position in between the particular and the general, it offers interesting possibilities for articulating an explicit approach to practice-based research; and second, there are reasons to think that it is in this part of the spectrum that research through design may have its biggest impact on how we think about design and designing.

Chapter 6, "Presenting," opens by revisiting the anecdote about examining design research. Using the ideas presented in the previous chapters, I present a different interpretation of what is going on and why the seemingly weak relations to theory in research through design are perhaps not weak but rather just different. Further, I discuss how the ideas about definitions made through design presented here, especially the notion of design programs, allow us to approach futures in and of design in a different way compared to when we start from practice. I discuss this as a difference between *futuring* and *presenting*, between redirecting practice and exploring alternative nows.

The book's concluding chapter takes a step back to comment on some of the more general aspects of transitional theory, such as the central role of definitions and examples in these accounts and what it means for how we address the inherent propositionality of the artificial.

Much as different prototypes are used to illustrate various aspects, potentials, and parameters of a design space, my discussion of transitional theory uses a set of examples located in different parts of this design space for design theory. This set is by no means conclusive, and the picture I try to show is still fragmentary.[1] Yet if some contours can be seen, some outlines can be traced, certain contrasts can emerge, then we can still answer the first, and at this point most important, question: if there is at all such a space for making design theory. And so this is the book's purpose: to expose enough evidence of a potential for making design theory in the context of research through design that others might consider taking a look.

This is an example.

2   Tactics

This book is about research through design, research by design, about practice-based, practice-led, and constructive design research and similar terms that refer to research where designing and making are a foundational aspect of the research process (cf. Joost et al. 2016; Koskinen et al. 2011). There are differences between these notions, but for the present purpose, what is more important is how they share an orientation toward designing and making as central to how the research process unfolds, and thus to what constitutes the core ways of finding out new things. For instance, the term "research through design" was initially proposed by Sir Christopher Frayling (1993) as one of three used to describe different relations between research and design, but has since been interpreted in various ways, as well as become the name of a specific research community and conference series. Consequently the precise meaning of the term has been equally mobile.[1]

While these research formats driven by design in many ways are just another member of the family of different ways of doing design, they are also different in that they to a significant degree are defined by an orientation toward creating new knowledge. Asking researchers who have done a practice-based PhD in design about the differences between practice and research, Katharina Bredies notes that "the deep reflection, the profound engagement with methodology, and the need for a highly structured approach is often radically new to PhD students in design in the early stages of their research. Likewise, the role that artefacts play in a research process is often entirely different: they do not need to function, but rather to provide explanatory power and serve as theoretical considerations in their own right" (Bredies 2016, 15).

There are several reasons behind the increasing importance of research in (and through) design. One key reason is that, as design problems become increasingly complex, the need for new knowledge in practice has become a more pressing issue. In the context of changing architectural practice, Michael Hensel and Fredrik Nilsson comment that "practice-orientation in research entails, among other insights, the realization that reskilling and thinking outside the established bounds is increasingly necessary to solve contemporary complex design problems at the pace of practice. ... There are two important factors that more than others seem to drive the need for research in architecture and contribute to the changes of architectural practice we currently experience, and which seem to influence practices of all kinds: *the increasing complexity* of architectural projects and *the digital technologies* and their rapid development" (Hensel and Nilsson 2016, xvi).

Reasons for changes in design with respect to research, however, can also be found within its institutional contexts and higher education. Whether one likes it or not, design education is increasingly treated, interpreted, planned, and evaluated as one of many different subjects in the university apparatus—and the history of design research in many ways reflects this (cf. Cooper 2016). Aspects ranging from curricula and pedagogics to the ways each discipline articulates itself and its "knowledge production"[2] are being compared across subjects, with funding being allocated based on performance. Thus, as much as we want the workings of research through design to be meaningful to design and designing, it would be naive to think that our institutional contexts and phenomena such as "academization" do not influence what questions are being asked, and how, in our field as they are in others.

Given how prevailing academic orientations tend to value theory over practice, what the notion of "theory" actually refers to in a domain inherently driven by practice, therefore, becomes quite important. If design in this context and condition does not even make a claim to theory development, then the old notion of design as a strictly *applied* art will take on a whole new meaning. Of course, many other matters of concern are also involved, such as what qualifies as a solid disciplinary foundation in the academic context in question, what qualifies as research, what forms of knowledge are privileged, and so on, but reducing theory in design to only a matter of applying more fundamental ideas developed elsewhere would be completely against the field's development since the 1950s.

Thus we have at least two reasons to take a better look at theory development in the context of research through design. First, we need to articulate and advance the way we understand theory in the context of design practices, a matter of increasing importance in light of the increasing external pressures and influences on design education. Second, while it is evident that research through design has real merit, both academically and professionally, and that it continuously gains traction as a research orientation, there are few, if any, detailed accounts of how this research actually develops its theory. While certainly exciting, it is also somewhat problematic that we are developing a consensus *that* something works while still not being able to articulate quite *how*. This book cannot hope to resolve such issues, but it is an attempt to engage with them head-on to learn something about what is at stake.

Anecdotal Evidence

Looking into what issues pertaining to theory emerge in this kind of design research, let's start with an example in which relations between theory and practice appear, at least from the outside, to be somewhat obscured and even weak. This anecdote stems from experiences and observations made in situations such as project and paper reviews, PhD thesis defenses, and similar situations of taking a step back and evaluating design research. Here I will use the PhD thesis as an example, since it illustrates well what examining a more complete piece of design research can be like. The story may go something like this:

In the account of a design research process of a PhD thesis, there is a rich body of theory in the early parts of the narrative. In the stages leading up to initial problem formulations and design conceptualization, one finds ample references to particular and developed theories, in many cases not from just one area but from many. In fact, one might wonder, when looking at the picture presented, how all these different theoretical orientations will be joined without serious conflict. Overall consistency seems hard to obtain, to say the least. Then, at some point, acts of design seem to take over, and the narrative puts aside the more theoretical concerns to deal with processes of making, leading up to a final description of the actual design output (be that this output is a still an open-ended process, a collection of things, or something else). A thesis of this sort will rarely return to the initial theories in the later stages. One might see a few references back to certain concepts presented earlier, but in general the overall process seems to have left that behind, leaving the reader with a rather vague idea of what actually happened to the complex theoretical foundation that was first proposed.

A typical response to this situation might be to think that it demonstrates an inconsistent, and in many cases therefore also superficial, relation to theory—especially if compared to how such matters are handled in other areas of academic work. With respect to issues of theory development in artistic and experimental design research, this also seems to indicate a weak connection between theory and practice, not only because of neglect but sometimes also because of explicit intent. Consider, for instance, the following remark by Bill Gaver: "More fundamentally, I am suggesting that, however valuable generalized theories may be, their role is limited to inspiration and annotation. It is the artifacts we create that are the definite facts of research through design" (Gaver 2012, 945).

Seen from the perspective of theory development being one of the primary objectives of research, concerns have been raised more generally in design, as here by Ken Friedman:

One of the deep problems in design research is the failure to develop grounded theory out of practice. Instead, designers often confuse practice with research. Instead of developing theory from practice through articulation and inductive inquiry, some designers simply argue that practice is research and practice-based research is, in itself, a form of theory construction. Design theory is not identical with the tacit knowledge of design practice. (Friedman 2003, 519)

Whether Friedman's analysis of the situation of theory-practice relations in design holds or not, an unsettling aspect of the whole thing is that some of the people who make these kinds of (seemingly problematic) accounts, and thus exemplify this relation to theory, are successful design researchers, who may have a significant influence on others' research. True, it will not suffice to say it is simply "implicit" or "tacit," but to assume that they do not quite know what they are doing with theory does not necessarily appear as the only alternative interpretation, perhaps not even the most likely. Further, since research through design often aims toward the conceptual, it often directly addresses issues related to interpretation, categories, values, and so on, making the assumption that the relation between theory and practice is simply weak even more problematic. And so what if this initial reaction of ours, even if in just a few of these cases, is completely misleading? What if we do not see what theoretical contributions are actually there because we are looking for the wrong kind of closure?

A starting point for this investigation is the idea that maybe it is not primarily the relation to theory per se that is the key problem in examples such as the foregoing anecdote, but instead some kind of structural mismatch between the character of the theories used and what design researchers use them for—and as a consequence, issues related to what we expect the theoretical impact and feedback to be like. In many ways, it is about exploring a notion of theory development close to Gilles Deleuze and Félix Guattari's idea about philosophy: "Concepts are not waiting for us ready-made, like heavenly bodies. There is no heaven for concepts. They must be invented, fabricated, or rather created and would be nothing without their creator's signature" (Deleuze and Guattari 1994, 5). To begin this inquiry, let us look at how theory is currently handled, and what tactics are in place to address it.

Three Tactics

In numbers, design research might be a relatively small area, but in terms of scope it is certainly not, as it ranges from art and design history to engineering and technology development—but importantly also from the analytic to the artistic. Throughout design's, and thus design research's, history, this scope has caused a range of tensions between the technical-rational, on the one hand, and the artistic, on the other. In many places that came to define what industrial design is, such tensions have been very present. Consider HfG Ulm, for instance, and the following remarks by Tomás Maldonado (headmaster) and Horst Rittel (professor in design methods):

Although my own cultural orientation was strongly marked at that time by Neo-positivism ... the presence of Adorno in Frankfurt represented for me, as it were, a contradictory intellectual stimulus. ... "The useless is eroded, aesthetically inadequate. But the merely useful lays waste the world," he once said to me in an attempt to cool my enthusiasm for the industrial culture of usefulness. ... These and other reflections in the spirit of Adorno, and later also Habermas, led me to examine the relationship between industrial culture and the culture industry, and to undertake a critical investigation of the role played by "design" in between these two realities. (Maldonado 1991, 223)

In retrospect, it becomes apparent that the HfG's [Ulm] most durable legacy was the endemic internal strife that kept the institution going. It is widely believed that the HfG was destroyed by the "policy conflict" between "designers" and "theorists." The truth is the exact opposite. The HfG stayed alive just so long as it remained a hotbed of discord. (Rittel 1991, 118)

Or, as in the remarks by Andrea Branzi:

In Ulm's case there has been the comic misunderstanding of treating designers as scientists, simply because they were talking about science. In reality, that hill was home to a group of extraordinary artists who, in the guise of inflexible scientists, were looking for beauty, that beauty so necessary to human life and so fragile and difficult to define and defend. (Branzi 1988, 42)

In design research, related historical tensions can, for instance, be seen between advocates of a "design science" versus ones who favored a "design discipline" (Cross 2001), not to mention in the significant difficulties encountered in resolving basic discrepancies between what is valued in professional, artistic, and scientific academic contexts (cf. Biggs and Karlsson 2010).

To make practical delimitations possible, this inquiry is located within the more specific context of what has been referred to as "research through design," "constructive design research," and similar terms (Joost et al. 2016; Koskinen et al. 2011), and domains such as industrial, product, interaction, or service design. The kinds of design theory discussed here therefore primarily concern questions related to basic concepts and structures tied to artistic foundations in design, and to the articulation of what it is that we think and do as we (indeed "we," as design is typically a collaborative activity) design. Examples of such basic concepts might, for instance, be form, material, function, use, user, and so on, but also concepts we use to explain how we structure design activities and their outputs, such as product or project, and the logic they bring to the structure of the creative process. I also want to place the discussion in the context of such design research because it so clearly bears traces of both art and science and therefore has to deal with the difficult conflicts arising from being in-between. From a research point of view, positioning oneself closer to either art or science would be easier, relatively speaking, but here we are looking for trouble, so conflicting views are something we're interested in. In what follows, I briefly introduce three different ways of addressing theory versus practice in design research, here called parallels, sequencing, and intermediaries.

Parallels

The first and perhaps most obvious approach to the gap between theory and practice is to acknowledge its existence but to build bridges across this divide. To put it bluntly, this approach approximates trying to avoid the problem and instead rely on existing research frameworks to create an over-all structure, keeping a clear distinction between the designing/making on one side and more theoretical accounts on the other. However, in practice this is still complicated to do, and one should not underestimate the effectiveness of this approach. I will call this tactic *parallels*, as it keeps the two domains parallel and largely independent from each other.

In its most straightforward form, the approach starts with an existing design practice and then adds a reflective layer on top of it, often in retrospect. It can, for instance, be seen in cases where a designer has been involved in a series of artistic or other development projects, building a set of works that is later used as a basis for a research project, such as doing a PhD thesis. The designer then aims to make the transition from artistic practice to research through elaborate reflection and theorization of these works. To simplify, what we get from this structure is in many ways a design practice combined with a research framework borrowed from (most often) the humanities or social sciences.

While this may result in interesting ideas and other relevant results, such parallels do not necessarily imply any significant changes to the way the actual designing happens. More importantly, however, this approach does not relate to theory as something addressed and potentially produced within the design practice as such. Rather, it largely relates to theory as something external. In a sense, what parallels do is to address the division of labor between designer and design theorist by bringing the two roles together in one overall project, but they do not necessarily challenge the division of the subject matter that such disciplinary habits enforce. Or, in other words, the research process tends to take on the character of the designer articulating and theorizing her own design work *as if* she were an (almost) external observer. Let us consider an example, how Maarit Mäkelä articulates her "retroactive approach":

I have written the main chapters only after the visual work process has ended, giving a retrospective glance at my artistic work process as an artist-researcher and placing my actions into the context of feminist theories. The speaker in my thesis is therefore the artist-researcher, who is reviewing her intuitive work process in retrospect.

... During the research process, the artist-designer reviews her artistic work process and the created artifacts from a retrospective viewpoint and creates a dialogue between her observations and interpretations on the one hand, and research literature on the other. (Mäkelä 2006, 176)

This example comes from artistic research, and while the approach may seem straightforward, it is still far from trivial to articulate its workings and contributions. Indeed, it is in many ways unfair to reduce Mäkelä's approach to a matter of keeping things parallel, as it is an elaborate account of how art and research interact and together create something she compares to a hermeneutical circle. At the same time, it is important to distinguish between the primary topic of this book—that is, design theory in general, and design's conceptual foundations in particular—and other, related, but also very different discussions in artistic research concerning what (kinds of) knowledge this research aims at articulating as it deals with issues related to nonconceptual content and experience. Consider the following statement by Henk Borgdorff:

We can justifiably speak of artistic research ("research in the arts") when that artistic practice is not only the result of the research, but also its methodological vehicle, when the research unfolds in and through the acts of creating and performing. ... This is not to say that viewpoints in art criticism, social and political theory or technology play no part in artistic research. As a rule they do play a part. The discourses about art, social context and the materiality of the medium are in fact partially constitutive of artistic practices and products. The distinctiveness of artistic research, nevertheless, derives from the paramount place that artistic practice occupies as the subject, method, context and outcome of the research. Methodological pluralism— the view that various approaches deriving from the humanities, social sciences, or science and technology may play a part in artistic research—should be regarded as complementary to the principle that the research takes place in and through the creation of art. (Borgdorff 2010, 46)

This gives us a different perspective on the reasons for keeping different parts of the research effort parallel to each other: while they speak to each other, they also remain separate because they are oriented toward fundamentally different forms of knowledge. With respect to such questions, design research may position itself almost anywhere on a spectrum between the artistic and the analytic, and so the relevance of the chosen position therefore depends highly on what the research in question aims to achieve. Obviously, all research acknowledges that there is a critical relation between methodology and what knowledge one may obtain, and in design research—with its span from art to science—this becomes particularly important, as it is sometimes hard to see precisely where on such a spectrum one is positioned and how that may differ from where others stand.

Consider, for instance, the differences between the earlier remark by Friedman and the statement by Borgdorff. Friedman states that "instead of developing theory from practice through articulation and inductive inquiry, some designers simply argue that practice is research and practice-based research is, in itself, a form of theory construction. Design theory is not identical with the tacit knowledge of design practice" (2003, 519). In contrast, Borgdorff states that "the distinctiveness of artistic research, nevertheless, derives from the paramount place that artistic practice occupies as the subject, method, context and outcome of the research" (2010, 46). Perhaps some of the differences can be traced to one of them focusing on theory, the other on research more generally, but it is nevertheless clear that while both of them seem to talk about practice and its relation to research, either they are not talking about the same kinds of practice (Borgdorff addresses artistic ones, while Friedman refers to the importance of inductive principles, hence likely advocating more analytical ones), or there is some confusion as to what kind of methodology is associated with what forms of knowledge.

There are many areas in which such uncertainty about what it is that we actually speak of is highly present in design research. Consider aesthetics, for instance. On a most general level, most of us would probably agree on some notion related to expressions and experience, likely using historically important ideas such as beauty or the sublime as reference points. But at some point, perspectives would start to diverge. Design researchers oriented toward history and the humanities would typically take off in directions related to art discourse, what art and artistic expression are and how they operate—and what it is to experience them. Researchers oriented toward the behavioral sciences would turn to psychology and sociology and what people experience in the encounter with things, aiming toward theories of human experience and how it structures the world as perceived. Looking in still another direction, the design researcher working with experimental design examples to investigate new materials, forms, and expressions might use the term "aesthetics" to describe the way these new things present themselves. As when saying, "What do you think about the aesthetics of this?" as a way of addressing the structure of, or basic reasons behind, their expressions. In many ways, this is all fine—as long as we understand that all these questions and answers are bound to their particular contexts, their particular methodological worldviews, and for the most part have little bearing on the knowledge generated in other such worldviews. This is not to say they exist in isolation or in a vacuum, but only that you cannot replace the artistic methodology of a given inquiry with an analytical one and expect to be answering the same questions, and vice versa.

Unless we understand that design research operates in a space between art and science, and this space actually affords considerable diversity, it is unlikely that we will be able to see that what we refer to as theory depends highly on what parts of this spectrum we want our theories to speak about. Indeed, it is crucial that we do not bring the evaluation criteria from one part of the spectrum to the results from another, as doing so will not necessarily tell us anything of interest and importance. Still, there are reasons for thinking about certain approaches to relations between design practice and design theory as a matter of parallels, and how certain aspects of research happen after making—though the two, in cases such as Mäkelä's, have been arranged in an unfolding circular pattern. Although such projects may range from the simplistic to the highly complex, we can think of their basic structure as matter of parallels, as they tend to leave the artistic/design practice fairly intact and the layer of theoretical articulation separate from it.

Sequencing

The next tactic shares many similarities with the first one, with one fundamental difference: whereas parallels keep making and theorizing separate, the one I call *sequencing* explicitly aims to bring them together. In particular, it aims to make theoretical notions influence designing in sometimes fundamental ways.

Typically, the theories that we apply to making are not themselves from the domain of design but from somewhere else. Significant examples of introducing theoretical frameworks into design come from areas such as psychology and sociology, from which theories for understanding and describing human perception and action were brought into the development of approaches such as user-centered design. There are also numerous examples of how philosophical positions have been introduced to conceptually ground experimental design practices. Let us take a brief look at some examples.

Design has a long history of borrowing conceptual as well as practical frameworks from the medical and behavioral sciences. Ranging from ergonomics to theories about attention and memory, there is a rich set of concepts, criteria, and contexts to build on when designing things for an intended user group and for evaluating to what extent they actually meet the users' needs. In Scandinavia, an early example is the Swedish Hemmens Forskningsinstitut (Home Research Institute), which was founded in 1944 to study and improve living standards in general, and women's working conditions in the home in particular.[3]

The HFI's approach was inspired by methods that had previously been used to improve workplace efficiency in industrial contexts. Research projects at the HFI ranged from calculating the optimal proportions of kitchens to minimize unnecessary movement, to studying work effort and different practices of preparing food. The institute's findings and recommendations played an important part in transforming Sweden's standard of living from among the poorest in Europe in the 1930s to one of the highest. The HFI's program also illustrates how user-centered design in Scandinavia has its origins not only in the design work more typically included in design history, but also in methodologies coming out of political efforts to change society through design. In that sense, the HFI is a precursor to contemporary socially and politically engaged design (cf. Ericsson and Mazé 2011).

Turning to contemporary research through design, we find approaches related to this early research on design and everyday things in, for instance, design research building on ideas from experimental psychology. Several design research environments have developed approaches based on the use of systematic laboratory experiments to close the gap between theory and design experimentation (e.g., Overbeeke, Wensveen, and Hummels 2006; Stappers 2007; Koskinen et al. 2011). For instance, the connection between theory and experiment in such projects can be developed through controlled studies of specific design variables in tests with human subjects. This structure of the research process allows design researchers to make significant use of certain theories throughout the design process while at same time keeping a space open for design experimentation. Using a highly iterative research process, more developed relations between theory and design

Rensning: borst....
m. m.
Beredning: hackning, skärning, pressning, passering,
stötning, malning m. m.
Varmmatlagning: rörning, vispning, stekning m. m.
Uppläggning, upphällning etc.

Diskning
Vid användning av lösa disklådor
»   »   » fasta, nedsänkta d.... dor

Bakning
Tillsättning av deg
Knådning av deg
Utbakning av deg

r

framkommit att husmödrar
lefekter i rygg, armar och
ned olämpliga arbetsförhål-
r t. ex. hårda golv, olämp-
förändring i arbetsställ-
lsen ordentligt, t. ex. små
alvuttagna steg m. m. Un-
g. svenska sjukgymnasters
letta.
rkas på flera olika sätt, och
eciella studier vid HFI.

nhänger med arbetsställ-
att man uppnår goda ar-
ten ansträngning och med
iken för arbetsställningens
ställande.
rett speciellt stora svårig-
kommer troligen att upp-
giska expertis, som sysslar
synpunkt. Undersökningar
därmed sammanhängande
ormning m. m. bedrives i
ns hantverksinstitut.
dessa undersökningar har
fter i huvudsak tre linjer:
enligt Douglas säckmetod
a utslag, men lämpar sig
toden är tidskrävande och

Fig. 5. Mätning av energiomsättningen vid tillsättning av d
på olika arbetshöjder medelst Douglas' metod. Genom anal
av utandningsluften, som uppsamlas i en säck, beräknas energi
omsättningen hos den arbetande.

Figures 2.1, 2.2

Photographs of archive materials: reports from Hemmens Forskningsinstitut (HFI), published
in 1947. The first (2.1) comes from a study of kitchens and cooking practices, document-
ing the experimental setup for measuring work effort when preparing dough at different
workbench heights (Bergström, Boalt, and Lindgren 1947). The second (2.2) comes from a
study of the design and ergonomics of different kinds of knives, showing prototypes made

	Skaver något i handen	12,2
	Holkskarven skaver i handen	13,4
Utan anmärkning		8,8
För utsvängd på ryggsidan och för kantig	Utan anmärkning	12,2
För utsvängd på ryggsidan och för klumpig	Utan anmärkning	10,2
Ryggsidan något för rak	Utan anmärkning	10,2
Utan anmärkning	Utan anmärkning	15,2
	Utan anmärkning	14,0
Utan anmärkning	Utan anmärkning	
Utan anmärkning. Bra stöd för lillfingret	Utan anmärkning	14,2
Utan anmärkning. Bra stöd för lillfingret	Utan anmärkning	14,0
Utan anmärkning. Bra stöd för lillfingret	Utan anmärkning	15,4
Olämplig. Vulsten skaver i handen	Utan anmärkning	14,6
Vulsten skaver något i handen	Utan anmärkning	13,0
Vulsten skaver något i handen	Utan anmärkning	13,4
För kantig	Utan anmärkning	12,8
	På det unders. ex. skaver slitsen för tången i handen	13,6
För kantig. Stödet dåligt utformat	På det unders. ex. skaver slitsen för tången i handen	12,2
Utan anmärkning. Bra stöd för lillfingret	På det unders. ex. skaver slitsen för tången i handen	15,2
Utan anmärkning. Bra stöd för lillfingret	Utan anmärkning	15,2

ett sådant (nr 12 och 16). Hus-
öd har hittills varit mindre van-
inte, att ett behov av en sådan
som redan denna provserie torde

esultat utformades ett antal plas-
rskärarskaft (fig. 7), efter vilka
ä (bok) tillverkades av de i den
esenterade företagen. Dessutom
l i direkt anslutning till nr 16.
st. olika modeller (nr 25—31;
rst fig. sid. 116), samtliga av
ilt beträffande tjockleken, än
skaft. Alla hade vidare väl av-
försedda med bakre fingerstöd.
fingerstöd — 2 st. (nr 25 och
kaftavskärning i anslutning till
28) med sned dylik i anslut-
gjordes utan främre stöd. Av
t. (nr 29) den ovannämnda, en-
k ökade upplagan av det tradi-
v typ nr 16, 2 st. (nr 30 och 31)
craftig snedavskärning i främre

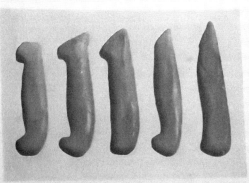

Fig. 7. Modeller, utförda i plastelina, till förskärarskaften nr 25, 27, 28, 30 och 31.

ändan. Dessa snedavskurna skaft, som alltså har ryggsidan framdragen över bladryggen, avser att hindra tummen eller pekfingret att komma i kontakt med bladet vid sådana arbeten, där man vill hålla så långt fram som möjligt för att få ett bra grepp. Vid flera skaft både med och utan främre fingerstöd gjordes nämligen enligt de utförliga försöksprotokollen anmärkningar på denna punkt.

123

Figures 2.1, 2.2 (continued)
in modeling clay that were used for testing (the next iteration of prototypes was then made in wood) (Carlgren, Nyberg, and Holme 1947). Thus two key aspects of user-centered design methodology can already be seen here: tests with users to obtain both qualitative and quantitative data, and iterative prototyping, where the fidelity and material quality of the prototype increase over time.

can evolve as the understanding of how the different design variables will have an impact on the test situation grows deeper.

Such basic methodology is sometimes combined with, for example, a philosophical framing that sets the basic conceptual orientations for the design process. An interesting example of such an approach is work on "embodied interaction" by scholars such as Kees Overbeeke and colleagues in Eindhoven, in which notions from the phenomenology of Maurice Merleau-Ponty and the ecological psychology of J. J. Gibson were used to form a design research agenda explored through a methodology combining design making and experimental psychology (see also Dourish 2001).[4]

An example that works with a different kind of theoretical basis, and philosophy rather than psychology, is Pelle Ehn's (1989) use of Wittgenstein's notion of "language-games" to articulate what prototyping a new (design) practice could be like, and how it works from a conceptual point of view. In these projects from the early days of Scandinavian participatory design, a key issue was how professionals could bring their expertise into the design situation when their knowledge is hard or even impossible to articulate in forms that could have an impact on the design decisions made during development. Instead of getting stuck in issues of representation, Ehn shifts the issue into participation and the problem of language into a question of how shared language is first established through language-games:

If designers and users share the same form of life it should be possible to overcome the gap between the different language-games. It should at least in principle be possible to develop the practice of design so that there is enough family resemblance between a specific language-game of design and the language-games the design of the computer artefact is intervening in. A mediation should be possible. (Ehn 1989, 116)

The result was a new kind of collaborative design, where prototypes are not only prototypes of technical objects but the very building blocks used to create new and shared language, in a sense moving toward prototyping a shared "form of life." Thus the process combined the use of philosophical notions to open up issues in new directions, and the concrete interpretation of these new directions through collaborative making.

Needless to say, this tactic I am calling "sequencing" has produced significant results in design research, and as it will continue to do so, it will remain a most important part of our repertoire. Still, trying to look critically at what this tactic brings, we need to ask if there are questions in design that such an approach might have difficulties getting at. One such domain seems to be issues pertaining to design's own foundations. For instance, there are few, if any, examples of how this tactic allows us to address and critically examine issues pertaining to the artistic foundations that still somehow also govern the designs developed. In a sense, while the psychological theories allow us to examine certain specific design variables, the project as a whole still depends on a design ability to craft something that makes sense as a whole and can be experienced as such. While the theories can be used to account for such wholes in more sweeping terms, it is difficult to get to the specific issues that the actual designing needs to resolve (cf. Djajadiningrat, Overbeeke, and Wensveen 2002). Similarly, while notions such as language-games provide a different foundation for how we relate to each other in and through making, they say little about the making as such; and even after decades of participatory design, we still struggle to make more precise accounts of, for example, the particularity of the expressions of these prototypes beyond ideas about how "unfinished" things encourage elaboration and discussion in ways that "finished" designs do not. Indeed, such "aesthetics of the social" remain a largely unresolved matter in design research.

Thus there seem to be limits to what aspects of design that sequencing speaks about, and these limits stem from what areas the theories originally engaged with. While this is not surprising, what is perhaps more important is that this also suggests a deeper issue, namely, that what we see here are basically various forms of applying theory with little chance of making the transition to actually developing radically new theory. Another indication that this might be the case is that design research only rarely develops new contributions to the basic theories it engages with—which in turn suggests that this does not automatically mean we are moving forward when it comes to questions about how to initiate a kind of "basic" research in design (as distinct from an "applied" one) that addresses design's own foundational issues. However, this is just speculation on my part. Given the efforts currently going into design research conducted along these lines, results may well suggest that this indeed offers a way forward for design theory also in a more foundational sense.

Intermediaries

The third tactic of interest to us here, which I will call *intermediaries*, aims directly at the tension between the general and the particular. Addressing questions about what kind of knowledge is needed, and produced, in design, scholars have attempted to articulate theories at different levels of abstraction so as to move them closer to practice. A historically important illustration is Christopher Alexander's (1979) pattern languages, which were intended to structure and support collaborative planning and development of housing and cities, and how this idea was later adapted in areas such as computer programming and interaction design (e.g., Löwgren 2007). This is related to what has been argued to represent a kind of intermediate-level knowledge in design research, that is, something that is "more abstracted than particular instances, without aspiring to be at the scope of generalized theories," as Kia Höök and Jonas Löwgren put it (2012, 23).

One of the most successful examples of how to orient oneself toward more intermediate levels of theoretical abstraction—although never really framed in this way—is the idea of specific form-languages, as in the instantiations of a particular design semantics or semiotics. There have been various versions of the idea that design decisions regarding form and functionality can be understood as a kind of language based on parts and rules for how they combine. In Swedish industrial design, the work of Rune Monö gives us an informative illustration: "The product's message is formulated in a 'language' that we see, hear or feel. This language consists of signs. Signs are the subject of semiotics. Within product semiotics, these signs consist of forms, colors, sounds and so on—in other words, elements that we usually associate with aesthetics" (Monö 1997, 21). Monö's book *Design for Product Understanding* (1997) is in many ways an instantiation—in the form of an explicitly laid-out form-language—of the idea of product form as something structured like language. As expressed by Klaus Krippendorff and Reinhart Butter: "Just as a journalist creates informative messages from a vocabulary of terms, so could a designer be thought of as having a repertoire of forms at his disposal with which he creates arrangements that can be understood as a whole in their essential parts and that are usable by a receiver because of this communicated understanding" (Krippendorff and Butter 1984, 5).

What is interesting in Monö's remark is how he suggests that issues traditionally understood as a matter of aesthetics can be addressed in terms of semiotics. Besides being a highly functional hands-on approach in a context aiming for the design of useful products, this is also an explicit answer to the complex question we briefly touched on earlier, namely, what designers talk about when they talk about "aesthetics." At that point, I suggested that a designer/researcher who is primarily engaged in making, and in the exploration of form, might use the term to quite simply refer to the way a certain thing presents itself, its expressions. And in many ways, this is precisely what Monö does here: explaining what we talk about when we discuss what and how a thing presents itself to a user. What is also important to note is that this form-language is tied to a particular kind of design (although it might become widely spread), to a certain aesthetics, if you wish. Thus it sits somewhere between the particular and the more general; it is more widely applicable than a given design (or family of designs), yet more constrained and context dependent than we would expect from a more general theory of aesthetics.

As such, it addresses a basic tension that design theory cannot escape: the issue of the particular versus the universal. Erik Stolterman described this as follows (see also Nelson and Stolterman 2012):

Within the scientific project, the focus is on regularities, mechanisms, patterns, relationships, and correlations with the attempt to formulate them as knowledge, preferably in the form of theories. The intention is to form theories that constitute knowledge that is valid and true at all times and everywhere. ...

... In contrast to the scientific focus on the universal and the existing, design deals with the specific, intentional and non-existing. Interestingly enough, dealing with design complexity involves almost fundamentally opposite goals and preconditions as does the scientific approach. This is especially true when it comes to the notion of universality. In design practice, the goal is all about creating something non-universal. It is about creating something in the world with a specific purpose, for a specific situation, for a specific client and user, with specific functions and characteristics, and done within a limited time and with limited resources. Design is about the unique, the particular, or even the ultimate particular. (Stolterman 2008, 58–59)

Taking a step back, this points to a basic difference in what we need theories in experimental design for compared to many other areas of research: whereas others look toward the universal for support and stability, design needs theories that support conceptualizing, articulating, making, communicating, collaboratively creating, and so on, something new and particular. Elsewhere I tried to describe this as a difference between aiming for abstract images of the actual versus creating concrete images of the potential.

Moving On

The previous sections have presented an overview of three established and in many ways highly successful ways of addressing different aspects of theory in design research engaged in making and experimenting. I have also, however, argued that there are matters that these approaches struggle with. As we move on and look for other alternatives and options, I would like to point to two further aspects of the research associated with these tactics. And (un)fortunately, they both relate to characteristics we typically do not want theories to have: temporality and contextuality.

If we start with the implications of context, it comes from the tension between the general and the particular. The tension between design's general orientation toward the particular and how theory aims to speak about the general is a foundational problem. We have seen different ways of addressing this tension, for instance, by developing situated accounts that do the job of theory in a certain situation but do not have the reach beyond the particular that we traditionally look for in theory development. Thus, one of the aspects of design theory that we might have to consider more carefully is to what extent we are dealing with situated knowledge, and what that means for how we understand the reach and scope of our doings.

The issue of situated knowledge is a complex topic in itself (cf. Haraway 1988); still, many of the questions asked here are quite basic. For instance, how do we balance the general reach of a term against its effectiveness and relevance in a specific context? Consider the problem of how we may easily end up with definitions of foundational terms such as "form" that do not transfer outside a particular context, thus making critical inquiry across such contexts more or less impossible, as there is little chance of talking about the same thing. Or, equally unproductive, that we end up with general notions that fail to address practice. Consider, for instance, how most academic discussions of what design *in general is* seem to have little or no impact on how actual designing happens and is communicated.

Obviously, that theories have properties related to reach and explanatory scope is an issue in all areas of research, but in our case, this is a foundational problem because of the tension between the particular and the universal. Perhaps this is not a matter we should seek to resolve in the sense of seeking to dissolve it, but rather something that calls for a more explicit articulation of the tensions between the particular and the general. I turn to this issue in the next chapter.

Another aspect that calls for more attention in the three tactics I have discussed is how our responses to difficult matters all seem to result in temporal solutions. While some of this can be understood as a consequence of how designing is an unfolding process, there is something important about how temporality matters here—ranging from the anecdotal example in the beginning of the chapter to the various forms of turn taking between making and theorizing discussed above.

It is difficult to define what design is,[5] but there are shared features among the family of definitions offered. In particular, definitions frequently refer to design's orientation toward the future, toward the currently nonexistent; what John Chris Jones expressed in his definition of design as "the initiation of change in man-made things" (Jones 1992, 6) or what Herbert Simon stated as "courses of action aimed at changing existing situations into preferred ones" (Simon 1996, 112). Thus, to make things even more complex for the prospect of theorizing within experimental practice, the basic tension increases further as we add another seemingly contradictory relationship: the one between inductive processes aiming to uncover what remains constant and stable, and design's general orientation toward change (cf. Nelson and Stolterman 2012).

The concern for change seems to drive designers toward methods: whatever the field may lack in terms of theory development, it certainly compensates for when it comes to methods. In terms of basic character, methods more obviously support processes of change, as they explicitly relate to the temporal and the unfolding, whereas theory traditionally builds on the stable and the constant. Another way, perhaps, of interpreting this situation is that methods offer a different relation between question and answer, between problem and solution, compared to the typical orientation of theories. Whereas we tend to want theories to rest firmly on the answering side of the equation, we are more comfortable having methods primarily engaged in the questioning part. And since designing, at least ideally, orients itself around problems and questions opening up something, *making* something, either we need to bring theory there, or else it may easily be reduced to tools for reflecting on the results.

Moving on, an idea to explore further might therefore be to what extent design theory is set up to be present when answering versus in what ways it is meant to support questioning. Again, this is not by any means unique to design research—but again, things become more hands-on in our case, the primary reason being how we aim to initiate change through design. Not leaving the world as is means that the questioning-answering relation is a matter of agency. We cannot articulate methods without certain central concepts: our design methods may be as unorthodox as anything, but if our work at the same time still relies on conservative definitions of foundational terms, these definitions will most certainly retain a fossilizing influence. Or in other words, we can be as inventive as ever when working with the design of a thing belonging to a certain category, but if the definition of the category itself is left untouched, then we will remain firmly within its frames. Indeed, I argue that this is one of the reasons why certain aspects of design remain so remarkably uncontested despite practice otherwise undergoing such significant change. Therefore I will return to the issue of definitions we use to articulate what kind of designing we are doing, and how such definitions can also be more sensitive to unfolding and temporality, in chapter 4.

3 Between

In what follows, I begin to look into how definitions are made *through* design. Starting with the question of what it might mean to redefine what designing is about, I intend to start unpacking tensions between the particular and the general to open up a kind of design space in between. In the previous chapter, we saw that this tension in some ways represents a fundamental problem to design theory. An alternative interpretation of that same observation—taking a design approach—would be to say that since this seems to be a serious conflict that needs to be negotiated, this is probably also a good place to start working.

In the research briefly discussed in the previous chapter, two basic ways of negotiating this tension stood out. The first used time and process to create a kind of oscillation between the two, moving back and forth between them, often associated with methodological notions about taking turns between action and reflection (cf. Schön 1983/1991). The second sought to position theoretical articulations somewhere in between what could be considered of general scope and what is intimately tied to a particular context.

In what follows, I try to phrase this issue slightly differently and instead aim at an account of what kinds of things we might expect to encounter in different parts of the spectrum between the concrete thing and a general theory. Trying to keep things simple and transparent, I work with very basic, almost trivial, examples. This approach means that the examples may not immediately appear as "real" theories. Yet examples such as the basic definitions discussed here are still the basic building blocks of theory, and if the approach I am sketching cannot deal with such simple examples, then it will certainly not cope well with more complex ones, either.

Anecdotal Evidence

The opening anecdote of this chapter is taken from a conference series called "Design and Semantics of Form and Movement" (DeSForM). When preparing my talk for the 2015 conference, I decided to make the first sentence of its mission statement the basis for the talk:

DeSForM is a Design Conference that speaks to the notion that the nature of things, the essence of what a fabricated object is, was about to be, and really should be, completely and fundamentally questioned, re-defined, and exploded.[1]

Being invited to give a keynote, I felt I should be able to, at least in principle, answer the question: "Okay, so you want us to *redefine the essence of what a fabricated object is*. How would one *actually do that?*"

Trying to understand and unpack this statement, I began with the mutual presence of both the concrete and the general. On the one hand, there were references to "the nature of" and "the essence of," which suggested a general claim; on the other, it was clearly also about actual things and "what *a* fabricated object *is*." If I was looking for the conflict between the particular and the universal, then it was certainly present in this one sentence.

The DeSForM's mission statement is bold and inspiring, and it is not the only one of its kind calling for action and change in design. Already at the beginnings of industrial design, questioning the nature of the fabricated object was central. In 1923, László Moholy-Nagy stated:

It is not enough to improve old forms. ...That is merely to give an old dress a new hem. ...
   ... The good object can offer only one unambiguous solution: the type. ...
   ... The Bauhaus attempts to produce the elements of the house with this economy in mind—therefore to find the single solution that is best for our times. It applies itself to this task in experimental workshops, it designs prototypes for the whole house as well as the teapot, and it works to improve our entire way of life by means of economic production which is only possible with the aid of the prototype. (L. Moholy-Nagy 1998, 302–303)

While there are obviously differences between DeSForM's present-day statement and the Bauhaus's of nearly a century ago, the similarities are striking. At a more superficial level, it is always the case that any given design expression also is a matter of the culture in, and through, which it is expressed. But there is also something more stated here: that we may actually redefine what design in general is through the making of new and different designs.

If we believe this is indeed possible, we need to ask how this works: what is it that we actually do when we say we want to fundamentally redefine what a fabricated object is *through* design? I will address this question by articulating an account of how it perhaps *could* be conceived.

Three Propositions

In what follows, I try to resolve, or at least to address, an example of the tension between particular and general as expressed in the design intent to fundamentally redefine what a thing is. The reason for choosing this particular statement is that it clearly has this tension while at the same time seems to having a bearing on how we in design tend to express ourselves in issues like this. I will sketch an answer in the form of three propositions.

1. *We make definitions through design.*

The first proposition is that we make definitions through design. The way we do so depends on a very basic way in which humans connect things and words, or concepts: what philosophers call "ostensive definitions." While far from trivial to account for in more rigorous academic terms, the basics are quite straightforward. Let us start with an example.

Consider how a chair defines the act of sitting, and how, therefore, designing a chair in a certain sense is a matter of defining what sitting is. When we make a chair, its form will define a certain intended bodily position, a certain act of sitting. If someone asks us, "What is sitting?" we can point to the chair, sit down in it, and say, "*This* is sitting." While the experience of sitting down in this chair is our own, it can also be shared, as when we invite the person asking us what sitting is to sit down in the chair. And we say: "*That* is sitting." In this way, we define a general term—"sitting"—through the concrete design of a given thing, that is, this particular chair.

However, we are not necessarily tied to this specific chair only, as we can bring another chair into the conversation and say things like "*This* is *also* sitting." In fact, it is this latter move that we often use to redefine what things are. Consider bringing a very different chair into the conversation, such as the "sitting device" made by Hans C. Mengshoel and Peter Opsvik, in which you partly sit on your knees to obtain a more ergonomic

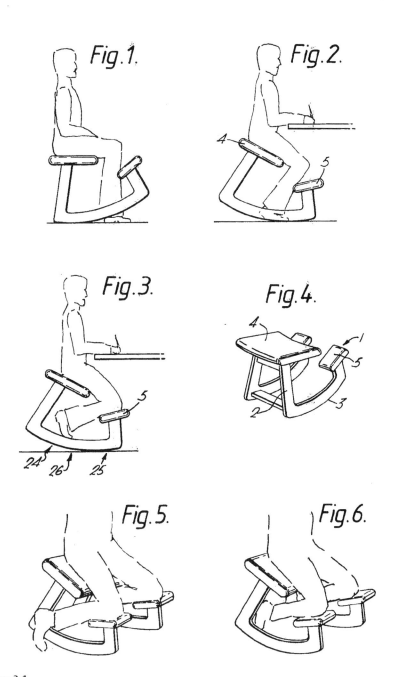

Figure 3.1
Illustration from patent no. US 4328991 A for a "sitting device" by Hans C. Meng-shoel and Peter Opsvik, 1982.

posture for the back. This is an example of how the act of sitting can be redefined through another kind of design. It is not necessarily a new definition replacing an old one, but rather a partial redefinition that allows us to expand the design space of chairs. Or consider Dunne and Raby's "Faraday Chair" (Dunne 1999, 104):

> The use of chairs to express prevailing values and ideas about design is well established. Chairs also echo the human body and can communicate new images of man. For example, the bean bag expressed the new informality of the 1960's. A Faraday Chair could provide a new image of the technological person: not of a cyborg fusing with technology, or of a master of technology, but of vulnerability and uncertainty about the long-term effects of the technologies now so enthusiastically embraced. …
>
> Although the final object was a smaller version of a day bed, requiring the occupant to adopt a foetal position, I kept the title Faraday Chair to suggest that, once electromagnetic fields are taken into consideration, conventional assumptions about everyday objects need to be re-examined.

If we question that this is indeed a matter of also fundamentally redefining what things are to us, let us consider another example: the telephone. Initially conceived as a hearing aid, the telephone became one of the first widely used communication technologies (cf. Ihde 1993). With the emergence of mobile networks, we quickly went from only having phones in fixed locations to having devices we carry with us, thus making a transition from phones as something tied to places to phones as something tied to people. Come the smartphone, and the phone's original functionality became only a minor part of what actually defines the thing in use as it now engages with a much wider notion of communication. And so, when I ask my kids what a phone is, they answer that it is called "a mobile," and they certainly do not have the same picture in mind as did my grandmother, should I have been able to ask her what a phone is. And then we have not even addressed what happened the first time Elisha Gray or Alexander Graham Bell presented their devices, saying, "This is a new device, I call it a …," then presenting initial definitions of what a telephone is. Thus I would like to argue that when we say things like "How tablets have redefined the rules of personal computing" (Bajarin 2013) or "Will Angela Ahrendts redefine luxury with the launch of the new Apple Watch?" (Pullen 2015), we actually mean just that.

In this way, we are able to connect general concepts with concrete things and literally make definitions through design. Although these ostensive definitions in many ways are part of our everyday routine, this is still far from trivial from a more philosophical point of view. This is, I believe, what Pelle Ehn aims at with the use of language-games in the participatory design process discussed briefly in the previous chapter. And so let us turn back to Wittgenstein for a moment:

So one might say: the ostensive definition explains the use—the meaning—of the word when the overall role of the word in language is clear. Thus if I know that someone means to explain a colour-word to me the ostensive definition "That is called 'sepia'" will help me understand the word.—And you can say this, so long as you do not forget that all sorts of problems attach to the words "to know" or "to be clear."

One has already to know (or be able to do) something in order to be capable of asking a thing's name. But what does one have to know? (Wittgenstein 1967, §30)

This remark points to at least two important implications we need to address if we are to maintain that we at least partly—and literally—make definitions through design. The first one is that since design is about making, probably only a part of what is important for us to define ever enters language. Consider the following statement, again by Wittgenstein (1967, §78):

Compare knowing and saying:

how many feet high Mont Blanc is—
how the word "game" is used—
how a clarinet sounds.

If you are surprised that one can know something and not be able to say it, you are perhaps thinking of a case like the first. Certainly not of one like the third.

If we return to our earlier example of the chair, it is clearly more like the third than the first. Certainly, I can explain in words what it is to sit, but for some of the (sometimes still crucial) nuances between different acts of sitting, I might not. Indeed, many of our design examples are like Wittgenstein's clarinets: when we aim to redefine what some *thing* is, what we offer is not a new description but a concrete design that *sounds differently*. Again, it is not unproblematic to say this—that this way of making basic definitions through design is not restricted to what we can express in words—but it is at the same time something that we need to acknowledge the importance of. Indeed, issues pertaining to ostensive definitions are quite present even in science, as once stated by Bertrand Russell: "All nominal definitions, if pushed back far enough, must lead ultimately to terms having only ostensive definitions, and in the case of an empirical science the empirical terms must depend upon terms of which the ostensive definition is given in perception" (Russell 1948, 242). Most contemporary scientists will not agree with Russell's project, but his remark still serves to illustrate how far this issue reaches into how we think about and make definitions.

Further, examples such as chairs may seem to suggest that while these definitions made through design are not precisely neutral and sometimes compete with each other (as when we discuss whether one chair is better than another), they can still be considered fairly straightforward things primarily concerned with matters such as utility, beauty, and so on. It is perhaps less clear that they also carry many other aspects related to the position and perspective of the one(s) making and using them. Even if we stay with such everyday matters such as sitting and chairs, we do not have to look far for examples that more clearly expose this: the chair at the end of the long table, the throne, the sedan chair carried by slaves, the execution device called the electric chair, and so on. If one doubts that even the simplest and most humble of chairs still carries with it aspects of both poetics and politics in its definition of what sitting is, then consider placing and using that chair in a context where one does not normally sit with the assistance of a chair but, for instance, sits directly on the floor, on one's knees. Even with the complication that these definitions include much more than one can express in words and that they are something given in experience, one may still try to maintain that a definition made through a design is neutral or ordinary—but what we actually look at when we think we see this is not neutrality but rather our own internalization of the values, norms, and ideas that constitute this particular context, this form of life.

Now, the second implication we need to address stems from Wittgenstein's earlier question: "But what does one have to know?" Let me turn to the next proposition, and to the contexts in which we make these definitions through design, and thus to another aspect of the relation between the particular and the universal.

2. *There is a space between design particular and design universal, and it ranges from addressing what a design is to what designing is.*

Trying to pin down what "particular" and "universal" actually refer to in design is much like shooting at a moving target. Instead of trying to make it stop moving, I will therefore allow the following to be a bit fluid, and when more precision is needed, I will turn to examples. Hopefully, it will then be clear why the precise locations of these terms are not that important, as this builds on relations rather than static positions.

Let us start with an example of how these targets move around. Basically, what we want to address here is the dichotomy between the particular and the universal in design in general, and more specifically to what extent it can be considered a spectrum. However, as we could see in our previous examples, what we may think of as particulars range from distinct objects (such as in the particular chair I pointed to when I said, "*This* is sitting"), to categories of products (as in the *Time* article about "how tablets have redefined the rules of personal computing"), and more (as when Gray or Bell first presented their devices, simultaneously defining a distinct object as well as what would become the category of things we call phones). This does not necessarily mean that our notion of what constitutes a particular is confused.

Consider, for instance, the term *product* and how we use it to talk about design and designing. When I say "this product," I can easily move between talking about a distinct thing and addressing the group of things it belongs to. To illustrate: even if I say, "*the* iPhone," it will be the context of my utterance that will help you determine whether I speak of the iPhone as a kind of product produced by Apple (as when I say, "When Apple first presented *the* iPhone"), or if I refer to a specific object (as when I say, "Could you please give me *the* iPhone"). This flexibility partly depends on the significant similarity across particular instances, but also on the pragmatics involved in trying to conceive of a continuity between, for instance, prototypes and manufactured objects—indeed, the very notion of a prototype of a product depends on this continuity, and therefore saying things like "*This* is *the* next product," pointing to a concrete thing, the prototype, actually makes sense to us. In this way, a term like "product" actually follows its moving target in a certain way (and, of course, sometimes also problematically so).

If we instead turn to the universal side, searching for counterparts to "product" as a kind of particular, let us consider the notion of *paradigm*. Even if we want to stay with a most general idea about what designing is, design is in many ways inescapably the design of *something*, often also for *someone*. Of course, we can approach design as all that which is constructed by human beings, thinking about designing as the bringing about of the artificial, but as soon as we start to talk about what that actually means (again in the light of a potential difference between making a theory of design and a design theory), we have to acknowledge context. Thus something more constrained will be more effective here. Consider, for instance, the earlier example when *Fortune* asked, "Will Angela Ahrendts redefine luxury with the launch of the new Apple Watch?" In an example like this, we would interpret luxury in relation to a certain context, knowing that there are also other interpretations of this general term. We would read luxury in the context of certain forms of consumption, but we would typically not associate this redefinition of what luxury is with what is referred to in expressions such as "We do not have the luxury of time"—although both are in some sense related to timekeeping.

To populate the spectrum between the particular and the universal with notions such as product and paradigm is also to avoid having to assume that this spectrum has definite end points that we can fix. This may or may not be the case, and it is therefore important that we do not implicitly assume that we can. However, keeping the ends of the spectrum open also reminds us that a notion such as "the universal" is inherently problematic. Design operates in a place of poetics *and* politics, and thus issues such as colonialism are still lurking if we think that certain values are "universal." Indeed, that certain ideas about what design is and does have gained global reach and impact is something quite different from assuming that such ideas also have universal value.

Now, if we start with the first part of the proposition, that there is a space between product and paradigm, we have something like the following to work with:

Figure 3.2

Starting to unpack this line, this empty space in between, let us follow the apparent fluidity of these terms and ask what happens as we move along this line. If we return to our previous example with the chair defining the act of sitting, consider what happens as we move between the different sides of that definition.

If instead of asking, "What is sitting?" we start by asking, "What defines this chair?" something interesting appears. If we ask a traditional furniture designer, the answer might be about how shape affords sitting, but perhaps even more so about how the combination of form and materials brings forth the distinct expression of this chair, how the different elements and materials meet each other, and perhaps also something about how it is the expression of a particular designer or the style of a certain brand. If we instead ask a materials engineer what defines this particular chair, her response might focus on material configurations and assembly and production techniques. And so on and so forth. In other words, if we try to position ourselves to look through these definitions in the opposite direction, what we see are glimpses of what the person answering considers design to be about.

This is just an initial hunch, but other examples suggest similar shifts as we start moving across the line. Consider what is added as we move beyond talking about the concrete thing in, say, an educational context. In a discussion at a degree exhibition, we might start by asking, "What is this thing you have made?"—but we would not stop there. Rather, we would continue to ask questions, not just about the thing or "product" as such but about the *project*: what was the process, what methods were used, what about earlier prototypes, and so on and so forth. Taking a step back to look at what is added to the conversation as we ask such questions, we see they somehow all relate to the relation between what a particular *design* is, and what kind of *designing* it is about.

Turning back to our line between product and paradigm, I would therefore add the following:

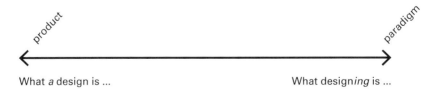

What *a* design is ...   What design*ing* is ...

Figure 3.3

And so here we have the second proposition: that there is a space between product and paradigm, and it shifts from addressing what *a* design is to what design*ing* is. Thus this is to be read not as a shift from design as a thing on one end to design as an activity on the other, but rather as the span between a distinct outcome and the overall orientation of the effort that produces such outcomes.

3. *This space between product and paradigm can be populated by projects, programs, and practices.*

Having suggested that there is a design space between the particular and the universal that design theory can operate in, and that this space has the character of a continuous spectrum, I started to populate its far ends with terms such as "product" and "paradigm." But perhaps the most interesting question is what we may find in the middle. This is very much the topic of the following two chapters, but I will start here by introducing a few key notions.

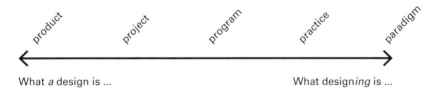

What *a* design is ...   What design*ing* is ...

Figure 3.4

Earlier I touched on the notion of "project" as a term we use to describe the immediate context of a given design. It is actually surprisingly hard to define what a project is, but a description would most likely entail aspects such as being an effort with given limitations in both time and resources, that a project ideally has an objective and thus could be understood as an effort to achieve something given, even though this objective might be quite vague at the outset. But importantly, a definition would also contain aspects related to how the project would be carried out, whether by plan, process, or other structuring principles. The term's ambiguity notwith-standing, the notion of project is central to much design work and thus of interest to us here in terms of how it add aspects related to what designing is, compared to when we address a product. Even within its limited scope, the project can tell us quite a bit not only about a given design but also about designing.

At the other end of the spectrum, the notion of *practice* soon emerges as crucial. If asked to define more precisely what designing actually is, we may turn to different design practices to explain matters further. Indeed, much professional design has at least one additional label suggesting what kind of designing it is, such as product design, graphic design, fashion design, and so on. Such design practices differ from each other not only with respect to the materials and contexts they work with, but to a significant degree also with respect to skills and ways of working—and often also values and conceptual orientations. Indeed, practices are "embodied, materially mediated arrays of human activity centrally organized around shared practical understanding" (Schatzki 2001a). One implication of this is that many, if not most, educational environments ask students to select their practice at the outset of their studies by choosing among different programs available. With respect to our interest in how this spectrum works—what this design space looks like—the notion of practice tells us much more about what *a design* is compared to a more general paradigm. For instance, we may learn about what kinds of designs such practices produce (such as houses, industrial products, or clothes), and how they do so.

At the same time, however, the notion of *a* design practice is quite fluid: at times it may refer to something individual, as when someone speaks about "my practice"; at others it refers to something done by a group of people; sometimes it is something quite general, as when we talk about differences between practices of fashion design and textile design; and in notions such as practice-based research, we refer to an even more general notion of practice. To complicate things even further, a single individual may easily use the notion of practice in all these ways within just one conversation. Thus the kind of inherent fluidity or mobility that seemed to characterize how we use the term "product" seems to apply also to "practice," and again this is not because we do not know what we are talking about.

To put practice into a spectrum trying to address structural matters in design theory might seem appalling from a philosophical point of view, where the basic distinction would instead have to be between theory and practice. Since this has been done many times, also in design, there are plenty of illustrations of what can be done if you start there—including the possibilities of opening up a slightly different space using Aristotle's third key concept, *poiesis*. The reason I want to move in another direction is that I am interested in what defines design and designing, and how such conceptual foundations are made and maintained. As such, it is not so much a matter of what (general) kinds of knowledge this is, but rather a matter of how design is conceptually structured through making, and thus that which grounds what Peter Schatzki refers to as the "teleoaffective structures" of practices, the "range of acceptable or correct ends, acceptable or correct tasks to carry out for these ends, acceptable or correct beliefs (etc.) given which specific tasks are carried out for the sake of these ends, and even acceptable or correct emotions out of which to do so" (Schatzki 2001b, 60–61).

What is referred to here as practice is not so much a position with respect to the theory-practice dichotomy but an interest in a more everyday use of the term, as when we talk about various practices of everyday life (cf. de Certeau 1984; Shove et al. 2007) in general, and in how we talk about different design practices in particular. What is crucial about such notions is that they point to something fairly "complete" as a whole (but to be honest, also often something we do not reflect much on, as it is *also* firmly grounded in effective ways of doing rather than ongoing critical reflection).[2] Whether we talk about a designer's practice or the ways a family structures its everyday life, "practice" refers to how the range of acts involved come together in certain ways, including the approaches or worldviews they embody. Thus to ask about practices of designing or cooking will have to include much more than descriptions of, say, sketching or frying, of making a prototype or a pasta.

Since both project and practice already are key terms in how we articulate what design is and how it is done, perhaps the most difficult term introduced here is *program*. Since this is also the part of the spectrum where I will argue that research through design may make its most important contribution to design, I will spend chapter 5 discussing the notion of program. For now, however, I will briefly introduce it to complete the picture proposed here.

In design, we use the term program perhaps most frequently when we talk about educational programs. While many educational programs in design make good use of projects, there are clear differences between the two. Whereas the purpose of a project can be to get a chance to experience a certain process or what it is to collaborate with a certain stakeholder and address a certain brief, an educational program aims at something more general. One way of putting it would be to say that *programs* function as educational frameworks that prepare designers for entering professional *practice*.

We may also encounter the term program as a description of the overall framework defining scope and purpose for a series of different but related projects. This is often the case with research programs, as when a funding agency opens a new research program with a call for project applications. Research programs can, however, also be of much smaller scale, but they denote something more general and open-ended than a project. Pushing the culinary metaphor to commit the crime of overly simplifying matters, we might say that if the *pasta* is our product, the *meal* is our project, and some form of *cooking* is our practice, then a program would be somewhat like a *cuisine* or a diet.

Returning to our initial question—what it would take to *redefine the essence of what a fabricated object is*—the answer emerging here is therefore not one of offering a new description of what design is or could become. Of course, various written articulations of what design is can help us see new perspectives, much as manifestos like the one from the Bauhaus can help set new directions. But to actually *redefine* design, we need to present new designs, new projects, and new programs that, as they come together, offer a different understanding of what designing could be like. Indeed, we can not redefine designing through words alone, as our definitions of design were never made in the realm of the written in the first place—designing has always been much more forcefully defined by ways of doing design and the concrete designs that these ways of designing produced. Indeed, to understand just how powerful and effective these definitions made through design are, we need to look deeper into their workings.

Structural Continuity and Precision

It seems that we can populate different parts of the spectrum between product and paradigm with terms such as project and practice. It also seems as if these terms are connected in certain ways, as when we say that a series of *projects* conducted within the frames of an educational *program* prepares the students for *practice*. We may therefore ask whether such examples of how we build continuity across the spectrum are accidental or not. So let us look at a few more examples.

Consider industrial design practice and how it has developed. First, we need to acknowledge that, like the ones discussed before, this term is also vague. Certainly we know what, for instance, industrial design is, but we also know that the variations in what such designers actually do are considerable. Still, if we look at its history, we clearly see that certain programs played a critical role in its becoming what it is today. Starting with industrial design's early history, we know that educational programs such as the Bauhaus, with its curriculum based on the basic course, the workshop training, and so on, influenced design education to the extent that what you would have learned in such courses still partly defines practice today. Or we may think about the program developed at HfG Ulm: the way it approached methods in design is now embedded in the foundations of how design work is structured[3]—and not the least in how this structure is communicated to other disciplines.

We could also look at more specific research efforts and how they have evolved over time. For instance, what we today call nuclear *programs* once started with the Manhattan *Project*. Or consider the ubiquitous computing project at Xerox PARC conducted in the late 1980s. In essence, it was about rethinking what a computer is, making a shift from computers considered as devices to computing becoming a widely accessible and increasingly invisible infrastructure that we access in a multitude of ways in all areas of human conduct. It was an attempt to rethink the way we live with computers, and as such a research effort instrumental in information technology's shift from distinct machines we use primarily at work to a kind of technological resource we access anytime and anywhere. The Xerox PARC project offers an interesting example of technology development, and I will focus here on what happens with its framing as it develops.

Initially, it was seemingly framed as a project, as can be seen in descriptions such as "The Testbed Devices of the Infrastructure for Ubiquitous Computing *Project*" (Weiser 1996; my italics), but already in the same document we can see a certain ambivalence, as in "The *project* constructed the three prototype devices. The Pad and Tab were funded partially by ARPA; the Board, the first *project* to be completed, was not" (my italics). Here the notion of project is used to describe both the overarching effort and the more specific experiments. If we look at another text, we see that this transition has been completed, and ubiquitous computing is now thought of as a framework rather than a project (thus much closer to what I have called a program): "Ubiquitous computing enhances computer use by making many computers available throughout the physical environment, while making them effectively invisible to the user. … Ubiquitous computing offers a framework for new and exciting research across the spectrum of computer science. Since we started this work at Xerox Palo Alto Research Center (PARC) in 1988 a few places have begun work on this possible next-generation computing environment in which each person is continually interacting with hundreds of nearby wirelessly interconnected computers" (Weiser 1993, 75).

This issue of terminology may seem a rather technical matter, but it is not the definitions of terms per se that interest us here; what is important is how the scope of a definition of what *a* design is, and what *designing* is, seems to be able to evolve and move from one part of the spectrum into another. In the case of ubiquitous computing, we have a redefinition of what computers are—how computers present themselves to us in and through use—that started with experiments and early prototypes, became a project, and then over time evolved to a point where there is now an entire research community working within this program (cf. the UbiComp conference).[4] Here, we can see a trajectory within the spectrum from the particular towards the general, as in how the notion "UbiComp" moves from being the name of project to becoming the label of research community. Importantly, however, we can also see that the experimental devices made to a certain degree still define what this kind of computer use can be like: the name is not the only similarity between the Xerox PARC Pad and the iPad by Apple. In other words, it is not only a matter of a term moving toward the more general, but more importantly about an assemblage of definitions made through design that is expanding across the spectrum between particular and general.

Examples of how initial experiments become projects, developing further into programs, and so on, tell us something important about the structure of this space.[5] At the outset of the chapter, I mentioned that many central terms in design are not easy to define in detail, and I used the term "product" to illustrate why this is not necessarily a matter of conceptual confusion but rather an effective response to the dynamics of its context. One might think that to do theory proper, one needs precise and stable definitions. While I agree with the need for precision, I think looking for stability over time to some extent will cause more problems than it will solve in design. (Design is, after all, frequently referred to as a discipline committed to *change*.)

Consider what would happen if we pushed this idea about stability in relation to the issue discussed here. Say that we asked for detailed and stable definitions of what is a project, a program, and a practice, including how the boundaries around them can be drawn and kept, so that we, in each case presented to us, would be able to say: this is a project, this is a program, and so on. While we would thus be able to achieve a certain precision for a particular case, we would intentionally—or unintentionally—also be stating properties of this space: that it is discrete. In other words, this stability would imply that products, projects, programs, and so on, are distinctively different things.

Based on how design makes these kinds of definitions through design, however, I would argue that, from a certain design theoretical point of view, the terms "product," "project," and "program" do not at all denote radically different things but rather represent variations of the same overall kind of effort or articulation: they are all *definitions made through design*. They vary because they address different parts of the spectrum between particular and general, but they all address the tension between these extremes, and thus they all contain some piece of what *a* design is and some other piece of what *designing* is. Indeed, what it so intriguing about phrases such as "how projects conducted within a program prepare us for practice" (as when we say that a project with an external partner conducted within an educational program prepares the design students for professional practice) is how the terms differ from, and belong with, each other, not how we isolate and separate them to give them individual meaning.

If this idea about how we achieve conceptual precision without really ever defining each term on its own, but rather by conceiving of them as part of a kind of space stretched out, seems awkward, let us consider a more everyday example: color.

I am quite certain you feel confident that you know what red is, yet when asked, "What is red?" what else could you do but point to things having that color and say, "Red is a color, and this is what it looks like"? You might also try to describe it in relation to other colors, stating that "red is a warm color" or "red is a primary color," referring not only to the particular color red but also to some frame for understanding what color in general is and how we culturally relate to it.

Advocating a more scientific understanding of precision, one might say that we actually can define colors as the wavelength of the light emitted or reflected. Certainly this allows us to create a kind of definition suitable for certain kinds of theories. Still, this approach offers an extremely particular understanding of precision, one that does not reach far into the concerns of design. For instance, it offers no real precision when it comes to our ability to address matters of aesthetics in an effective way. To illustrate, consider the following expression (cf. Merleau-Ponty 1968):

a sea so blue only blood would be more red.

Now, substituting blue and red for certain wavelengths in nanometers would not necessarily help us understand this expression at all. The expression itself, on the other hand, holds significant poetic precision (cf. Hallnäs 2010).

When it comes to color, we are also able to handle the fluidity of what is being referred to. For instance, we are used to handling disagreement about whether a given thing has a certain color or not: borderline cases such as when one person thinks something is green, and another thinks it is blue, are not rare.[6] In everyday life, we rather effortlessly understand that these terms have a fairly stable center but that their boundaries are often shifting, even on an individual level. Another example of such fluidity is when we consistently say that a white house is white during the different lights of sunset, first tending toward yellow, then just after sunset turning light blue. Of course, we see that the color is changing, and we can recognize the time of day or atmosphere in a photograph or a painting—but we still think that the white house is white and nothing but white. Most importantly, none of this makes us think that we do not know what color is, or what the different color terms actually refer to. On the contrary, we are quite certain about what both "color" and "*a* color" are.

The conceptual structure and precision of the definitions I have introduced and discussed are, in a metaphorical sense, similar to "color." It may seem odd that they become precise in terms of difference and relation, rather than what can be articulated when we isolate them from each other, looking for each notion's "essence"—but this, more than anything, is a habit of mind, a matter of what we normally look for when asking about what something is. The example of color clearly shows that we are equally capable of understanding what something is on the basis of difference.[7] And so what I am suggesting is that asking for the difference between project and program is in some ways, metaphorically, like asking for the difference between red and blue. Pushing the question, asking what is really a project, we can make the move of defining it in a manner similar to how we would define blue as emitted or reflected light of a certain wavelength, that is, stating properties of projects pertaining to scope, duration, resources, results, and so on—but like wavelength, this would be a definition serving only certain purposes and not necessarily providing any relevant additional precision when it comes to understanding what a project in general is about with respect to design*ing*. Because to be creative, we also need friction:

> The more narrowly we examine actual language, the sharper becomes the conflict between it and our requirement. (For the crystalline purity of logic was, of course, not a result of investigation; it was a requirement.) The conflict becomes intolerable; the requirement is now in danger of becoming empty.—We have got on to slippery ice where there is no friction and so in a certain sense the conditions are ideal, but also, just because of that, we are unable to walk. We want to walk: so we need friction. Back to the rough ground! (Wittgenstein 1967, §107)

The reason for our terms being fluid is not that we do not know how to properly define them, but because they are, in practice, defined on the basis of difference and where in this spectrum they are located. While this certainly makes them difficult to handle in some ways, it also means that they allow us to move and develop; being approached through difference rather than static criteria, they are already prepared to cope with continuous change. In the next chapter, I look further into the idea that certain definitions in design have to be inherently unstable to have a fluidity that allows them to stay open for an unfolding design process.

4   Making Definitions

In the previous chapter, I discussed how the dichotomy between the particular and the general can be conceived as a design space—as a spectrum ranging from what *a* design is to what design*ing* is—and how this space can be populated by notions such as products, programs, and practices. I also tried to show that while such notions may not be terribly precise from a more analytical point of view, they do not necessarily point to a conceptual confusion on our side, that we don't know what we're talking about. On the contrary, I argued that their fluidity, their *inherent instability*, actually helps us to address the characteristics of this spectrum and its structure, and how to stay open for the ways designs and designing develop over time. If this space were discrete, then more stable definitions would be useful; but since it seems rather to be a continuous spectrum, like a color spectrum, more fluid notions based on difference prove much more effective.

Several objections can be raised based on the examples I used. One of the first would probably be that the definitions I address are too simple to make the case. The objection might be something along the lines that of course the thing X defines what "a phone" is—that is because "phone" in that sense is just a name for X. In other words, my argument is merely a conflation of the distinction between defining and naming. But there is more to this than differences between defining concepts and associating names to things. To dig deeper into the matter, however, we need to move on to more complex notions, and more elaborate ways of making definitions.

In what follows, I address the making of definitions of more general terms, of the kind of concepts we use to articulate what design*ing* is about. The terms I use as primary illustrations are "form" and "user." Besides being both general and complex notions, they are also relevant because they are used across many different areas of design. But above all, they are interesting because of the role they play in expressions of what we think design is all about: one of them for expressing *what* it is that one creates when designing, the other for *whom* the design is intended. Indeed, in the cultural context of my work, Scandinavia, these two terms play a central role in many descriptions of what designing is: as when design is understood as "form giving,"[1] or when one of the hallmarks of Scandinavian approaches to design is said to be that they are "user centered."[2]

Looking into how these concepts have been and can be defined, I also use some of the key ideas brought forward in chapter 2 about temporality and context. Temporality emerged as an interesting aspect of how theory is addressed in practice-based design research, evident in existing tactics such as sequencing. In the previous chapter, temporality was clearly present in how the precise meaning of terms such as "project" move around, strengthening the initial idea that this is something our design theory needs to account for. In chapter 2, aspects of context came forth as critical in the tactic referred to as "intermediaries," that is, the articulation of theoretical structures that sit somewhere between the particular and the general: more widely applicable than a given design (or family of designs), yet more constrained and context dependent than we would expect from a more general theory (as in the difference between *an* aesthetic and *a general theory of* aesthetics).

I will inquire into the structure of more complex definitions through the making of these two examples, "form" and "user." With these examples, there are two main issues I would like to address. First, I want to look into the implications of using stable and static definitions in design. Second, I want to prototype what corresponding "unstable" definitions might look like as a response to the issues arising from stability, and how such definitions can be made as precise as static ones in the context of design and designing.

But let me first start with a short story.

Anecdotal Evidence

In 2008 I was part of a project called *Investigating Form* (*Undersöka Form*) led by Christina Zetterlund and Jan Norrman at the Nationalmuseum,

Stockholm, Sweden (Zetterlund and Plöjel 2008). Our brief was to explore the museum's understanding of form as expressed through its exhibitions and collections. The results were presented as an exhibition: "*Examining Form* was a project in which the designers Johan Redström, Matilda Plöjel, Zandra Ahl, the artist Markus Degerman and the choreographer Malin Elgán have been invited to give their personal interpretations of the museum and the collection of applied arts and design. The works created for *Examining Form* dealt with the interpretative role of the museum, its approach to design and history."[3]

In my time at the museum, what emerged to me as perhaps the most distinct aspect of how form was defined was not so much what objects had been selected but how they were presented. The entire context was built around a particular act of appreciation, an act that seemed to be basically the same whether the object in question was a painting, a sculpture, or a power drill. The act itself is best described with an illustration: a person standing, looking at an object from a distance, the object framed—as in placed in a cabinet or on a podium.

In the exhibition that followed, I tried to probe this act and its boundaries by using as simple and minimalistic interventions as possible. For instance, aspects of appreciating objects in terms of "pure" form got additions in the form of "dirt," as in the case of a walking aid equipped with a worn bag used to collect cans for recycling. Another addition was to add a chair to sit on, identical to the one to look at, offering the viewer a chance to reflect on the two different ways of appreciating a thing simultaneously.[4] The image shown in figure 4.2 is a mock-up used during the process, and because of various regulations, the final implementation was slightly different, with the chair "Ant" by Arne Jacobsen positioned in front of a glass cabinet containing another such chair.

The added chair traveled an interesting path during the course of the exhibition, from initially being interpreted not as part of the exhibition but as a chair in general to use for rest, to finally ending up with a sign similar to what could be read on all other objects in the exhibition: "Please do not sit." The primary reason was that the chair got broken after a while, but the trajectory still tells us something interesting about the power of context: after a while, this object also became subject of the same ordering principle, with a similar sign to confirm it. It seems as if the particular acts of appreciating "form" that this (kind of) context builds on will always have a much

Figure 4.1
Photograph from the design exhibition at the Nationalmuseum, Stockholm.

Figure 4.2
Exhibition sketch of two chairs.

more determining role than any object brought into that context could ever have (cf. Zetterlund 2013).

If we paraphrase Ludwig Wittgenstein's question, this time about form instead of the color sepia: "Thus if I know that someone means to explain [form] to me the ostensive definition 'That is called ["form"]' will help me understand. … One has already to know (or be able to do) something in order to be capable of asking a thing's name. But what does one have to know?" (cf. Wittgenstein 1967, §30). In a way, what museums (and other similar contexts) do is to answer precisely this question, "But what does one have to know?" The answer is not complete and of course there is a much larger context also determining the meaning of terms such as "form." Nevertheless, what the museum does, by means of how it has been designed—how we are led into its exhibitions, through the way its content has been curated and how it is presented to us, how we are meant to approach and appreciate these objects, and so on—is to provide

Figure 4.3
Photograph of the added chair from the exhibition. Note the two signs.

a particular context for making certain ostensive definitions possible (cf. the origins of the term "exhibition," from the Latin *exhibere*, "to hold forth, to hold out").

At the museum, we can see that answering a question such as "what is form?" is not only done through particular acts of making ostensive definitions, but importantly also through structuring the way such acts can happen. Once you are in this setting, and a sign or someone says to you, "This is form," you will not only see a thing but also experience a particular way of seeing, of approaching, this thing: the object and the act of appreciating it, together ordered in a particular way by the exhibition. Because the objects are placed on a podium rather than in the hands, in a cabinet rather than in a kitchen, with a sign saying "Do not touch" rather than "Please use," and so on, these objects will be made to appear to us in certain ways. To use Kant's terms, they are presented for the purpose of a "disinterested pleasure."[5]

Obviously there is much more to form than is present in the elaborate but still basically ostensive definition that the museum exhibition can be said to be, and we may raise the concern, "But form is much more than this!" But such objections are more like saying, "Color is *more* than sepia: it can also be like this, or this," than saying, "*That* is *not* a color." The difference between the two is crucial as we try to understand how these definitions are made.

Form

In what follows, I explore further how form is understood, and defined, in design. In chapter 2, I used the notion of product semantics and form as a kind of visual language to illustrate how design practice seems to resolve complex conflicts between the general (as in a general theory of aesthetics) and the particular (as in the aesthetics, the expressions, of *this* thing) by means of forming frameworks, such as programs, that seem to exist somewhere in between. There I quoted Rune Monö: "The product's message is formulated in a 'language' that we see, hear or feel. This language consists of signs. Signs are the subject of semiotics. Within product semiotics, these signs consist of forms, colors, sounds and so on—in other words, elements that we usually associate with aesthetics" (Monö 1997, 21). While Monö's main interest here is how to think about the ways a given design

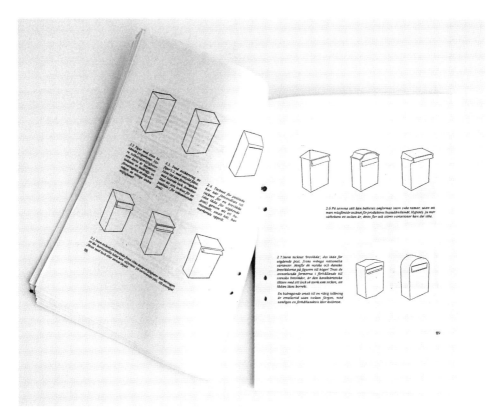

Figure 4.4
Photograph of unpublished teaching manuscript by Rune Monö for Umeå Institute of Design, "Design för att förstå: Designestetik med inriktning mot semiotic, 1995-08-31."

communicates what a product is and how it is intended to be used, we also learn several things about form, such as that it is distinct from color and sound, and it is one of the elements building these "product signs."

However, to understand how fundamental form is to the making of these signs, one needs to see the illustrations in Monö's work: how certain "gestalts" come about as the result of the ordering of visual elements, shapes, volumes, figure-ground relations, and so on. In this way, certain gestalts come to be considered primary "signs" for a given product category, so that whenever we see a certain form, we immediately recognize it as a mailbox, a hammer, or a car. Now, while these signs may be specific to this particular framework or cultural context, what is more general is this way of understanding what form is. In fact, it is an understanding that extends forward to the present, as well as backward to the very origins of industrial design.

Let us start with a textbook example. In *Thinking: Objects; Contemporary Approaches to Product Design*, by Tim Parsons, the first chapter, "Perception," offers a section titled "Reading Form," which "deals with our perception of form and some of the tools designers use to imbue their products with meaning" (Parsons 2009, 32). Here Parsons states that "products communicate to us through visual language. Like spoken and written words and sentences, this language can be split into units and studied" (32). Again, we learn that form is something visual, and its organizing principles can be approached in a way similar to language in general, and in some cases even to how a given message can be packaged in commercial communication in particular, as when Parsons remarks: "Form has become a tool some designers are using to generate recognition for themselves as brands. By feeding the press with images of consistently similar-looking products designed for different manufacturers, they define a set of forms that become identified as their own" (44).

Now, if we instead start to move backward in time from Monö and toward the origins of these ideas, we may encounter the paper "Product Semantics: Exploring the Symbolic Qualities of Form," by Klaus Krippendorff and Reinhart Butter (1984), in which they argue:

In its broadest sense, design is the conscious creation of forms to serve human needs. It sharply contrasts with the habitual reproduction of forms (4)

Just as a journalist creates informative messages from a vocabulary of terms, so could a designer be thought of as having a repertoire of forms at his disposal with which he creates arrangements that can be understood as a whole in their essential parts and that are usable by a receiver because of this communicated understanding. (5)

Thus, between Krippendorff and Butter in 1984 and Parsons in 2009, we see not only extremely similar ideas but almost identical descriptions of what form is. Such articulations, however, are much older than this and were to a significant degree already in place at the beginnings of industrial design as we now understand it. In 1938, György Kepes wrote:

As the eye is the agent of conveying all impressions to the mind, the achieving of visual communication requires a fundamental knowledge of the means of visual expression. Development of this knowledge will generate a genuine "language of the eye," whose "sentences" are created images and whose elements are the basic signs, line, plane, halftone gradation, colour, etc. (Kepes 1969, 197)

In his main work, *Language of Vision*, originally published in 1944, Kepes develops these ideas further:

To perceive a visual image implies the beholder's participation in a process of organization. ... Here is a basic discipline of forming, that is, thinking in terms of structure, a discipline of utmost importance in the chaos of our formless world. Plastic arts, the optimum forms of the language of vision, are, therefore, an invaluable educational medium.

Visual language must be readjusted, however, to meet its historical challenge of educating man to a contemporary standard, and of helping him to think in terms of form. (Kepes 1995, 13)

Thus, from the early days of industrial design to the present, we see a remarkable consistency when it comes to definitions of form as something visual, whether two- or three-dimensional. The foregoing examples also share other characteristics, such as a strong orientation toward communicating a given intent or purpose, with a corresponding focus on guiding intended interpretations and "making sense" through the use of conventions, iconic or in some other way standardized form-elements. Even if such orientations vary, it seems fair to conclude that form here has been given a stable and nearly static definition as something visual in two or three dimensions with an element-whole structure that can be compared to how language works.

Critique

Perhaps the most obvious question arising from the remarkable consistency across time (especially in light of all the other changes that design has seen in both scope and orientation) is to what extent this stability has been considered problematic. As we search for such critique, an intriguing pattern emerges. Let us look at a few examples.

The first place to start looking is "new" areas of design, typically articulated in terms of difference to existing and established ones. The UK Design Council's RED initiative presented the notion of "transformation design" using descriptions like the following: "Shaping behaviour rather than form. Design has historically focused on the 'giving of form' whether two or three dimensional. Transformation design demands a shaping of behaviour—behaviour of systems, interactive platforms and people's roles and responsibilities" (Bruns et al. 2006, 26). Two things are worth noting here. First, form is again understood as something visual. Second, the term is used to refer to what, in the authors' view, design *used* to be about. In other words, what this remark tells us is that the prevalent visual notion of form was unable to support further development in the direction that "transformation design" was aiming. Instead of form being redefined in relation to a new context and orientation, it is part of the "old" framework that the new approach differentiates itself from.

Let us look at another example, this time from C. Thomas Mitchell's *Redefining Designing: From Form to Experience*: "It is now becoming clear, in view of the large number of award-winning designs that have failed the test of use, that the design community's criteria for successful design differs radically from that of design users. … design itself needs to be redefined in terms of peoples' experiences, instead of in terms of objects. This static geometrical criteria of the design of the industrial era must be abandoned in favor of a focus on the dynamic, multisensory experiences of design users" (Mitchell 1993, 131). Here we see a similar argument with respect to form: that it is something visual, and it fails to support the design issues at stake in the "new" approach to design argued for. Again, this is not a unique example: in Andrea Branzi's (1984) history of Italian New Wave design, *The Hot House*, the first chapter is titled "From Form to Reform."

We can also move back in time and find related concerns in situations when design aimed in a new direction. This is an example from Otl Aicher, reflecting on the legacy of the Bauhaus in the context of HfG Ulm:

Is design an applied art, in which case it is to be found in the elements of the square, the triangle, and the circle; or is it a discipline that draws its criteria from the tasks it has to perform, from use, from making, and from technology? … The Bauhaus never resolved this conflict, nor could it, so long as the word art had not been rid of its sacred aura, so long as people remained wedded to an uncritical platonist faith in pure forms as cosmic principles. (Aicher 1991, 126)

Of course, the geometrical forms that Aicher points to at the Bauhaus are not necessarily identical to the general "geometrical criteria" that Mitchell critiques—but what is more interesting than whatever the differences might be is how very similar the critical remarks are. Thus what we have is not only continuity over time when it comes to design definitions of form, but also a continuity in the critical concerns for things falling outside this notion.

Perhaps the most important aspect of this critique is the central role of how the notion of form fails to support the development of design in new directions, and how other terms have to be introduced alongside "form" to expand the scope of design beyond the primarily visual, and to differentiate the new concerns from the old. It seems there is a conflict between the stabilization of the definition of form and the development of design in new directions.

Now, if the solution to this issue was simply to add another concept to account for whatever new aspects or dimensions of design are now necessary, then this would not have been much of a problem at all. The trouble is, however, that some of these basic concepts—like *form*—remain central to how we understand and do design. It is therefore necessary to critique it not only by adding options for differentiation but also by inquiring into what stabilizing mechanisms make it so remarkably resilient.

We need to understand how our definition of "form" come about not only because it seems reluctant to change (in a time when significant change is necessary) but because we, on a more basic level, need to start unpacking which characteristics of a given design theory support development and which ones stall it.

Stabilization

To account for why this particular understanding of form has been able to survive such significant changes to what design is and does is far from trivial, and what I can offer here are only initial ideas about where to look for answers. However, I have three suggestions for stabilizing mechanisms (and a fourth one to be addressed in the next chapter). The first one is the central importance of images in design, and how this continuously enforces the visual. The second one is how we fail to recognize the difference between concepts developed to account for *what is* and what is needed when articulating *what becomes*. Much related to this, the third one is that we confuse our own design programs with what other disciplines understand as general theory.

Images as Definition The first reason why this definition of form has been able to sustain itself has its origins in the ways our visual culture works in general, and how an image of something can be considered to be a definition of what that thing is (cf. Redström 2012, 2013).

The basic idea is that the image of a design works much in the same way as does the museum setting in terms of structuring a particular way of appreciating and approaching the thing in question. A design depicted in an image is, of course, different from a painting hanging on a wall or an object on a podium, but the similarities are striking: you cannot "use" the thing, only look at it from a distance; you cannot manipulate the thing, only passively observe it; and so on. Thus what features of the thing stand out, that come to the foreground in this particular act of appreciation, are all more or less restricted to two- or three-dimensional visual expressions. Essentially what is contained within this notion of form corresponds more or less exactly to what can be captured in an image (or, in the case of the three-dimensional, what can be put on display), and vice versa.

Now, compare the ratio of designs first encountered through images to designs first encountered through use in the wider sense of the word. The difference is staggering: not only do design competitions, magazines, and so on, primarily work with the image material, but even in situations when we actually go to the store to get the "real" thing, we often first encounter it through the visual material on its packaging. As Guy Debord once put it: "The spectacle cannot be understood as an abuse of the world of vision, as a product of the techniques of mass dissemination of images. It is, rather, a *Weltanschauung* which has become actual, materially translated. It is a world vision which has become objectified" (Debord 1983, 5). Try this: go into a supermarket and look around, taking note of how much food is first presented to you through images, and how much of it you actually see directly.

Let us consider another example. In his discussion of the influence of the Barcelona Pavilion by Ludwig Mies van der Rohe, Jonathan Hill states: "The Barcelona Pavilion is not the same as its photograph. It is an icon of twentieth-century architecture for the wrong reasons, not because it is a building with a subtle and suggestive program but precisely because it existed as a photograph and could not be occupied. Between 1930 and 1986, while the Pavilion did not exist, it was probably the most copied building of the twentieth century" (Hill 1998, 139). Further, Hill argues that "the major currency in contemporary architecture is the image, the photograph not the building" (137), and "architects are primarily interested in form, a condition reinforced by the architectural photograph" (150). Hill also makes the connection to acts of appreciating art, as in "Ironically, an architect's experience of architecture is more akin to the contemplation of the art object than the occupation of a building" (144).

Again we see how much of what defines this understanding of form is not a matter of how it is articulated in words but a matter of how it comes to expression in the acts through which we encounter it:[6] as when approaching and appreciating the thing as if it was a piece of art, as in what we encounter when we see an image of it, and so on.[7] In this way, the use of images to document, describe, and communicate what design is simultaneously also reinforces an understanding of form as a static visual expression.

Confusing Concepts for What Is with Concepts for What Becomes   To further unpack this tendency to confuse and use concepts meant to describe *what is* to apply also to *what becomes*, let us go back to the time when industrial design discourse began to form. In the early days of design, many basic courses were taught not by designers but by artists. For instance, if we think about the presence of Vasilij Kandinsky and Paul Klee at the Bauhaus, it is not surprising that an understanding of artistic expression based on visual form takes center stage. However, the very decision to work in a place like the Bauhaus suggests that there was also a strong concern for moving beyond earlier conventions into new domains. And so perhaps we should also turn toward the more general context of art theory at the time. If we do, we find some interesting examples. In a letter from 1935, László Moholy-Nagy made the following comment:

I have been back to the Stedelijk Museum time and again, and I know it now: my paintings are not yet ripe for mass exhibition. ... There are hardly any people yet who want to see the tentative worth of this new language. They'll complain about monotony; they'll scorn the repetition of the same form and color problem in new combinations. Nowadays visual gratifications have to come fast like the response of a jukebox, or the click of an amateur camera.

   This is bitter because the real purpose of exhibiting my pictures is to make the spectator grow slowly as I grew in painting them. What a long way to go! Most people I watched at the exhibition looked like oxen. (S. Moholy-Nagy 1950, 216)

In the study of his work by his wife Sybil Moholy-Nagy, there is also a remark regarding another series of artistic experiments:

But in spite of seemingly countless variations, around 1944 the light modulator came to an end as part of Moholy's development from form to motion and from pigment to light. Because even the light modulator remained a static painting, no matter how dynamic its composition. The spectator was still compelled to view it passively like any other work of art born from the Greek tradition. (216)

It is worth noting that some of the key issues discussed earlier in the chapter also surface here, such as the occurrence of the expression "development from form to …" in the second quote. Another issue we have encountered before in the opening story: how the museum setting, in particular the acts of appreciation it is built on, effectively prevents anything moving outside this frame to gain traction: "The spectator was still compelled to view it passively like any other work of art born from the Greek tradition." In the first quote, we see traces of how Moholy-Nagy was trying to expand the format from within, to incorporate time and becoming in the work: "The real purpose of exhibiting my pictures is to make the spectator grow slowly as I grew in painting them." It seems, however, that such attempts to address aspects of becoming failed to be recognized—something that Kandinsky also commented on in *Point and Line to Plane*: "The tendency to overlook the time element in painting today still persists, revealing clearly the superficiality of prevailing art theory, which noisily rejects any scientific basis" (Kandinsky 1979, 35).

One way of understanding the reason for these conflicting views is that while the artists were interested in the *becoming* of the work of art—and had privileged access to what this becoming was like, as they were very much part of it, being the actual creators of the thing in question—the art theorists worked only with what was, in the end, present to them. Of course, aspects of the making of these works might have been of interest also to the theorists, but nothing was fundamentally challenging their view that these new paintings were *still* paintings, objects that can be hung on a wall and appreciated from a distance like the others already there.

We are therefore talking about two different matters: one using form to understand the becoming of a thing, the other using it to describe something existing in front of us, as a piece hanging on a wall.[8] At first glance, this may seem like a version of the shift from product to process in design and art; but while sometimes overlapping, the distinction between analysis and projection (between what exists and what becomes), is something quite different. Articulating design in terms of product or process is still primarily a matter of describing what something *is*. As Sanford Kwinter put it: "For the poverty of what is today collectively referred to by the misnomer 'formalism,' is more than anything else the result of a sloppy conflation of the notion of 'form' with that of 'object.' The form problem, from the time of the pre-Socratics to the late twentieth century is, in fact, an almost unbroken concern with the mechanisms of *formation*, the processes by which discernable patterns come to dissociate themselves from a less finely-ordered field. Form, when seen from this perspective, is ordering *action*, a logic deployed, while the object is merely the latter's sectional image, a manifest variation on an always somewhat distant theme" (Kwinter 1994, 65).

Consider, for example, the relation between a piece of music and a performance of the same: although the performance itself is all about process, and there is no resulting physical "object" like a painting or an installation, we can still address the piece as something that exists. Take John Cage's *4'33"* as an example, in which the actual performance of the musician is basically to be completely silent. The experience of a performance of the piece is, however, not at all one of complete silence. Instead the act of listening turns toward the ambient sounds and thus to the question of musical material, of what sounds constitute a musical performance. Now, while the notation is very sparse indeed, and each performance is indeterminate, bound to context and in many ways a matter of music as an unfolding process, we can still address *4'33"* as an *existing* piece of music (and there was also a time when we could not address it as such, i.e., before it had been *made*). We can refer to *it*, this *it* has a name, and we can even analyze *its* form ("why three movements?"). Thus whereas the distinction between product and process typically refers to the (temporal) character of the "thing" we are talking about, the distinction between what exists and what becomes is a matter of its ontological status. While the two are related and sometimes overlap, they are not the same.[9]

Confusing Programs for General Theories   If we look at, say, art and design history, it is reasonable to think that such a discourse has an interest in developing general frameworks that support analysis across a wide range of instances. For example, we would be interested not only in articulating the expressions of a certain piece of art or design artifact but in doing so in the context of a more general understanding of how such expressions have developed over time and across various cultural dimensions. Most of the time, our primary interest would be not in the specifics of a given work only but in how and in what ways this particular piece is an instance within a more general category—such frameworks ideally not only having the scope of small collections of individual works but also working across periods of time, styles, and schools, and so on, to allow us to account for and articulate developments over time.

To do this, key concepts need to be stable. Indeed, a reason to keep a notion like form tied to visual expression is to be able to study changes in such expressions over time. And to work with such a stable notion of form is not at all problematic for this purpose, because it is meant as a concept for describing things that *are*, and not meant for things *that could be.*

Now, if we turn to something like Monö's product semiotics, it could be read as a kind of analytical tool that allows us to articulate and account for the way products make sense to people. But Monö's basic objective is not analysis; it is design. His framework is not the design historian's account of the development of visual form over time or the analysis of features that could be said to carry certain ideas about artistic expression across instances, but rather a practical tool for designers to project their intentions into the future. To make this possible, Monö needs to move away from accounting for what exists and instead "speculate" about what might become. Undoubtedly, the framework creates strong connections between the two: since people *are used to* interpreting visual form in this way, using a similar form will most likely make people interpret a new thing in a similar way. But there is a fundamental difference between analysis and design, and as we have seen in the earlier examples, what happens over time is that the price for this strong connection between *what is* and *what becomes* is that the latter conforms to the former when we use concepts made to account for what exists to also project what may become.

In the short term, confusing the two might not necessarily stall development. Indeed, when the kind of product semiotics that, for instance, Monö advocated first came around in industrial design, it was probably a highly effective and productive program that supported new design expressions. It is when we look at what happens over time that the more problematic aspects emerge, and the risk of fossilization becomes apparent.

And so this is the mistake we make: since what we have in front of us seems so similar to the stable concepts of the general theories that other disciplines depend on, we forget that our counterpart is not meant to perform the same task, and what we have, and need, is really only meant for a transitional "now." Our framework was never meant to account for what is and its relation to what was; it was not meant to be a general theory in the sense other disciplines think of such things. It was the scaffold we needed to make sense of a vast range of possibilities open for us: for navigating the potentiality of what could become, not the actuality of what became. But over time, it shifts from being a transitional and temporary foundation, and when it does, it is no longer a support for development but a framework for making sure things stay the same. It becomes history, not in the sense of a reflective and critical understanding of the past and its influence on the present, but in the sense of a now confined to repetition.

An Unstable Definition

If we return to the conflict between the particular and the general, and how to construct theory in a way that supports an unfolding process rather than precise descriptions of what has already been made, we learn from the earlier examples that the generality and precision needed in design are not necessarily the same as those needed in analysis. On the contrary, we can even anticipate severe implications if we confuse the two. I have traced some of these issues to notions of stability, arguing that we cannot afford stability if it comes at the price of static definitions that cannot support development. I have also tried to show that the ways we make definitions such as that of form are not so much a matter of written articulation as they are a matter of certain acts framing and ordering what it is that we perceive and relate to as form. In other words, it is not in theory presented as written discourse about form that we find its most powerful definitions. Rather, such definitions are to be found in the images sustained by exhibitions and educations, museums and magazines, and so on.

And so let us sketch an alternative way of defining form for design. The intention is to look for something that has a certain inherent instability to it and can be made through design in a way similar to the more simple definitions addressed in the previous chapter.

Looking for places that could accommodate such instability, an intrinsic openness, my suggestion would be to aim for the intended acts of appreciation and approach. I have several reasons for this, the primary one being what we could see in the earlier examples: how the institutionalization of such acts (e.g., the ways images are used) seems to exercise such power that whatever is brought into that context becomes subject to that particular way of approaching it.

But we also have another basic reason for looking in the direction of acts of appreciation. If we trace notions of form backward in history, we will at some point probably end up with Aristotle. While far from easy to fully understand, some aspects of form in Aristotle's treatment of perception and action in *De Anima* are worth noting here. To simplify, we might start with saying that form is the way "matter" builds things:

We are in the habit of recognizing, as one determinate kind of what is, substance, and that in several senses, (a) in the sense of matter or that which in itself is not "a this," and (b) in the sense of form or essence, which is that precisely in virtue of which a thing is called "a this," and thirdly (c) in the sense of that which is compounded of both (a) and (b). (Aristotle, *De Anima*, 2.1)

With respect to perception, he then makes the following definition: "By a 'sense' is meant what has the power of receiving into itself the sensible forms of things without the matter" (2.12). While our understanding of how perception works has evolved considerably since Aristotle's time, the basic idea here is still quite ingenious: since we cannot have a mountain in our head, what happens when we perceive a mountain is that the mountain's form, not its matter, is received. Quite literally: *in-form-ation*, the receiving of form through one's senses. Though it may not have been of specific interest to Aristotle, this is of some importance to us: that what form is to us ultimately depends on what it is that we perceive. In other words, what "form" refers to is not only determined by the perceived object per se but in a concrete sense codetermined by the ways it is experienced, by the specific acts of perception involved. In this way, different acts of approaching and appreciating something will require correspondingly different conceptions of form—and vice versa (indeed, note the difference between "form" and "sensible form" in the quotes from Aristotle).

Using this as a start, I would therefore suggest a definition of form that incorporates both object and act and is located not in either but in the relation between them:

Form = def. that (expressive structure) which emerges in the associated acts of perception.

The first thing to note here is that any instantiation of this *general* definition, that is, a more *particular* notion of form, will not only be about a certain kind of structure or composition but also be tied to certain associated acts of perceiving it. For instance, if I talk about a "circular form," I am talking not only about circles per se (unless I am referring to a circle as perhaps Plato would) but also about a certain act of perceiving, of *seeing*, circles. So because of the typical acts involved in watching a movie, if I say that the form of this movie is based on a circle, then you would probably think of a temporally circular or repetitive structure with no obvious beginning and end, rather than something literally showing a circle all the time.

Or try this: ask someone to think about a basic form and draw it. Likely you will get something like the following in response (fig. 4.5):

Figure 4.5

Then ask a musician in a rock band to think about a basic form and play it. Perhaps you will get something like figure 4.6 in response.

Figure 4.6 shows a diagram of a common basic musical form, the 12-bar blues (the roman numerals refer to the scale degree of the chords' root note). For an actual musical illustration, try, for instance, "Red House" by Jimi Hendrix, "Equinox" by John Coltrane, or "I Got You (I Feel Good)" by James Brown.

To generalize, whereas "form" refers to the way matter builds a thing (whether a painting, a product, or a piece of music), we refer to it also with respect to what emerges in the associated acts of perception and appreciation (perception is used here in its wide sense, not by any means restricted to passive observation).

"Associated acts of perception" refers to the acts that one would normally expect in connection with the genre in question, such as *reading* a book, *listening* to music, or *looking* at a painting, that is, the acts typically privileged by the practices constituting the normal context of the work. But we could also aim for acts outside these normal ones, and importantly this definition asks us to be explicit about whether we do build on such established frames of reference or not—and thus what these intended acts actually are. The definition will also make it clear when there is a conflict between what kind of form we are concerned about and the context where

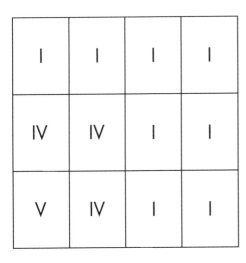

Figure 4.6

it is presented, as when the acts it relates to have no real presence in that context. A trivial example is the impossibility of expressing the temporal form of things through static images, but we can also think about what aspects of the form of appliances and other primarily useful things meant to be part of everyday practices are lost when such things are presented as though they were art objects.

"That (expressive structure) which emerges" refers to what stands out, what comes to the foreground in experience, as we encounter the thing through these acts. In particular, "that (expressive structure)" refers to what it is that we, as designers, primarily aim to create or make possible. To create the conditions for this something to emerge is, practically, what "to give form to something" is.

To give a practical example, consider making a definition of form in the context of bicycles as that which emerges in the act of riding: inviting a person to go for a ride, saying, "To understand and appreciate the form of this bike, the beauty of its geometry, you need to ride it." Then bringing forth another bike, and then yet another ...[10] Now, compare this to the experience of attending a museum featuring bikes, or of browsing a bike magazine.[11]

In the previous chapter, I used color as a metaphor to describe the conceptual structure of the space of products, projects, and programs, and we can see similar structures here, as well; the general definition of form "as that which emerges in the associated acts of perception" corresponds to saying something about what is "color." Then the concrete set of acts framing a more particular notion of form (e.g., as the visual shape of some thing) would correspond to what "*a* color" is. Moving beyond the basic frame of human experience, stating—along the lines of Aristotle—that "form is the way matter builds things" would in the case of color be somewhat like saying something about what light is (without framing it in terms of how humans experience it). Like color, form is a spectrum, and to approach it only through a specific set of acts of perceiving it, inherited from nineteenth-century European visual art, is very much like pointing to a set of green objects and saying, "This is color." It's not that it is not true; it's just that it is only a very limited set of what it could be.

While this new definition states what form is as precisely as any other definition we have looked at so far, it differs in how it requires us to be explicit about how it depends on its context in a much more direct way.

And while I have discussed aspects of context, I have still stayed within a specific cultural context (i.e., the one I'm situated in), which means that we are looking at only a part of the whole spectrum here—if we would instead start from a cultural lens different from mine, then other examples of cultural expression, other aspects of what form is and how relations between things and experiences are framed, would come into view. Our own articulations are tied to the position we inhabit, and the way to handle this is not to seek arguments about universality that would legitimize speaking on behalf of all others, but rather to be more careful not to stand in the way of what others have to say. To look for the *one* definition of a notion like form in design is structurally much like trying to find the *one* distinct color that will define for us what color is.

This is why it is crucial that we work with a kind of definition that requires us to add something to it: in this case, that it is left open with an explicit requirement that we specify what the associated acts of appreciation are. As this definition requires us to specify what these acts are, it gains specificity when we complete it, and thus we push the definition toward the particular. This is crucial, as it exposes something about where we, sometimes literally, stand as we approach a given design, and it reminds us that our definition is in some sense situated even as we speak about general matters.

User

Another term of some importance to how we understand and articulate what design is and does is the notion of a user. We use this term for a number of things, including to describe general design orientations such as "user-centered design," as well as to define the scope of specific methods such as "user studies" or a "user evaluation." While the wide application of the term "user" certainly affords a range of critical inquiries, I focus here on aspects related to the issues found in the previous example of form, and in particular the confusion of concepts for articulating what *is* for ones meant for what *becomes*.

User-centered design comes in many variations, and while details of accounts may differ, some basic traits are more or less consistently present. To get started, consider the ISO 13407 definition of human-centered design:

Human-centered design is characterised by: the active involvement of users and a clear understanding of user and task requirements; an appropriate allocation of function between users and technology; the iteration of design solutions; multidisciplinary design.

Central to user-centered design is the idea that involving users in a design process is perhaps the most effective way to ensure that the resulting design does what it is meant to do. As such, user-centered design is essentially both an affirmation of design as giving form in the sense of what was conceived at the Bauhaus and a forceful rejection of the same: what is kept is the idea that there is something we might understand as (more or less) optimal form that perfectly fits its context and intended use; what is rejected is what defines the basis of this fit.

To illustrate this combination of affirming and rejecting, consider the following two examples from IDEO and the Bauhaus respectively. Let us start with the words of one of the most successful examples of a business built around user-centered design, IDEO:[12]

It's a process that starts with the people you're designing for and ends with new solutions that are tailor made to suit their needs. Human-centered design is all about building a deep empathy with the people you're designing for; generating tons of ideas; building a bunch of prototypes; sharing what you've made with the people you're designing for; and eventually putting your innovative new solution out in the world. ... And you'll know that your solution will be a success because you've kept the very people you're looking to serve at the heart of the process.

Central to this statement is that the key to success is that the design process will ensure that the design solution will fit its intended context. Let us now look at Walter Gropius's manifesto for the Bauhaus (Dessau) from 1926:

In the conviction that household appliances and furnishings must be rationally related to each other, the Bauhaus is seeking by systematic practical and theoretical research in the formal, technical and economic fields to derive the design of an object from its natural functions and relationship. ... An object is defined by its nature. In order, then, to design it to function correctly—a container, a chair, or a house—one must first of all study its nature; for it must serve its purpose perfectly, that is, it must fulfill its function usefully, be durable, economical, and "beautiful." (Gropius 1970, 95)

To better see the similarity with the statement from IDEO, let us substitute "use" for "nature": "An object is defined by its use. In order, then, to design it to function correctly—a container, a chair, or a house—one must first of all study its use." We can also add the notion of iterative prototyping:

"The Bauhaus workshops are essentially laboratories in which prototypes of products suitable for mass production and typical of our time are carefully developed and constantly improved" (Gropius 1970, 96)—and substitute "collaborative" for "Bauhaus" with respect to what kind of workshop we are using: "The collaborative workshops are essentially laboratories in which prototypes of products … are carefully developed and constantly improved."

There are, of course, many important differences between the two statements, and the shift from "nature" (understood as a kind of normative, or indeed universal, ideal) to "people" as the defining context of design is by no means a small thing. Indeed, this shift is one of the key issues driving the critique of form discussed earlier. But however people centered this shift from nature to people as the defining context of a design may be, it must nevertheless also be understood in the light of design failing to achieve its intended function or fit. Earlier in the chapter, the quote from Mitchell regarding the need to focus on experience rather than form clearly points in this direction—and his book *User-Responsive Design: Reducing the Risk of Failure* (2002) states it even more clearly. In other words, the critique of form as the primary orientation for design is not only a matter of values but in many ways also an extension of the same trajectory set out by Gropius, that "to design it to function correctly—a container, a chair, or a house—one must first of all study its nature; for it must serve its purpose perfectly" (Gropius 1970, 95).

And so the shift we can see can be interpreted not only as a matter of putting people first but also as a consequence of finding out that only technical or functional concerns do not fully account for what the use of something is, and thus what one needs to know to make something serve its intended purpose must also include what people do. Elisabeth Shove and her collaborators comment that "even a brief review of what has become of user-centered design shows how keen designers have been to appropriate and adopt methods from disciplines as varied as psychology and anthropology, bending them to the task of understanding and delivering what users and consumers want. Innovative techniques of observation, body storming, shadowing, immersion and rapid prototyping … are reputedly effective in identifying 'latent' consumer needs" (Shove et al. 2007, 129).

This development is perhaps especially visible in areas of complex products giving rise to more complex interactions in use, such as housing (as

in the examples of Mitchell), or as in the following examples from when
interaction design gained widespread traction in the late 1990s:

A key question for interaction design is: how do you optimize the user's interactions
with a system, environment or product, so that they match the user's activities that
are being supported and extended? One could use intuition and hope for the best.
Alternatively, one can be more principled in deciding which choices to make by
basing them on an understanding of the users. ... In particular, it focuses on how to
identify users' needs, and from this understanding, move to designing usable, useful,
and enjoyable systems. (Preece, Rogers, and Sharp 2002, 5)

It is from work in cognitive psychology over the last several decades that we have
come to appreciate that we cannot just impose designs on users. People are active
parts of the system, and because they are much less predictable and less well understood than the computers and other technological parts of the system, they require
even greater study and understanding. (Hackos and Redish 1998, 15)

The intimate coupling of user research and development is, however, much
older than this; Roy Sheldon and Egmont Arens, for instance, published
Consumer Engineering: A New Technique for Prosperity in 1932.

One could argue that the similarities I am pointing to across these widely
different examples merely reflect the basic idea that design, unlike art, is
always about designing some*thing* for some*one*, and thus the issue will surface whenever a new design area is being formed. But I am after something
much more specific here, related not so much to what design is as to how
it is meant to happen. What we see in the foregoing examples is significant
development in terms of what design turns toward, what is included in the
scope of its concern, and so on. At the same time, however, we see that at
least one idea seems to survive this development in fairly intact form: the
idea that studying *what is* forms the basis for understanding *what could
become*, the idea that there is something we could understand as "optimal
form" that perfectly fits its intended use and context and that the design of
this something needs to be based on studies of nature, people, users, and
so on.

The User Category Mistake
The historical development toward present-day user-centered design is
therefore also the development of a category mistake: because we do not
recognize the difference between concepts meant to describe what is and
concepts that we use to project what becomes, we think that the user we
can study is also the user that we define through our design. But it is not.

People, not users, inhabit the world. Unlike a person, a user is someone defined in relation a thing: to be a user is to be a user of something. A person is not a user from the start but may *become* a user: turning to a thing, inviting it be part of her lifeworld, making it hers, deciding to start using it for some purpose ... becoming a user as she starts to use it. This cannot happen if that something is not there for her to use. Thus a first indication that something is wrong here is the ways that notions of user, people, human, and so on, are used almost interchangeably in many accounts of user centeredness—like the one from ISO 13407 we began with: "Human-centered design is characterized by the active involvement of users."

And so we might respond: well, of course it takes some kind of use for a user to truly exist, but what we are talking about here are *intended users*, that is, real people whom we can talk to and work with, and who eventually, when the design process is ready, will have a product that they can actually use. To speak of "user-centered design" is just shorthand for this process—an argument we might reinforce by saying that it also just reflects the symmetry in the distinction between, on the one hand, the people making the things, the *designers*, and, on the other, the ones using it, the *users*. In other words, while we admit that we might be talking about two different categories—existing and intended users (one referring to real group of people, the other being something that might, or might not, exist in the future)—this is okay from a pragmatic design point of view, as the former will eventually turn into the latter.

And so let us look into whether this is a feasible response or not. Inquiring into the relations between intended and actual use, we find little support for this position. On the contrary, we find significant evidence of the opposite. Earlier in the book, I used the example of the telephone. Consider what Don Ihde says about its use:

Only sometimes are technologies actually used (only) for the purposes and the specified ways for which they were designed. Two interesting examples of this have been the typewriter and the telephone. Both were originally intended as helps for impaired persons. ... What was to become their extremely important set of social uses ultimately entailed little of the original designer intent. (Ihde 1993, 116)

Related remarks can be found within a range of different frameworks. Here is one from sociology by Madeleine Akrich:

For some time sociologists of technology have argued that when technologists define the characteristics of their objects, they necessarily make hypotheses about the entities that make up the world into which the object is to be inserted. Designers thus define actors with specific tastes, competences, motives, aspirations, political prejudices, and the rest. ... A large part of the work of innovators is that of "inscribing" this vision of (or prediction about) the world in the technical content of the new object. ... To be sure, it may be that no actors will come forward to play the roles envisaged by the designer. Or users may define quite different roles of their own. (Akrich 1992, 207)

Indeed, the more problematic aspects of this understanding of use and users have been expressed also within design. Some fifteen years after the Design Methods Movement, John Chris Jones made the following comment:

But there is a hidden cost, a severe one, which has only recently become evident. It is that of inflexibility, over-specialization, the realization that this "plastic world" of homogenized, cost-reduced products is increasingly unalterable, un-repairable, and imposes upon us (from its stabilization of the larger scale of functions) a life, an obligatory way of using what is made, that is felt as coercive, not satisfying, with decreasing outlets for individuality. The lesson is obvious, though how to apply it is not: do not stabilize functions. (Jones 1988, 221)

More specifically targeting the user's role as envisioned, or inscribed, by design, Anthony Dunne states:

This enslavement is not, strictly speaking, to machines, nor to the people who build and own them, but to the conceptual models, values, and systems of thought the machines embody. User-friendliness helps to naturalise electronic objects and the values they embody. For example, while using electronic objects the use is constrained by the simple generalised model of a user these objects are designed around: the more time we spend using them the more time we spend as a caricature. (Dunne 1999, 30)

First, it is conceptually problematic to confuse an *existing* group of people using some existing thing in ways we can study, and the *idea* about use and users that we as designers use to project future possibilities. Second, this leads to quite foundational problems concerning what it is that design actually does, or tries to do. I have argued that this is a trajectory toward "user design," that is, design where the processes through which people turn into users are in focus and where the explicit aim is to work with the results of this process, that is, how use and user should turn out—and as such a breakdown of the distinction between *what* it is that we design and *who* is going to use it (Redström 2006).

In many ways, Richard Hamilton's idea about the future of design presented in 1960 in the UK Design Council's (then called the Council of

Industrial Design) magazine *Design* is still disturbingly to the point, and it is worth recalling it at some length:

Design in the fifties has been dominated by consumer research. A decade of mass psycho-analysis has shown that, while society as a whole displays many of the symptoms of individual case histories, analysis of which makes it possible to make shrewd deductions about the response of large groups of people to an image, the re-searcher is no more capable of creating the image than the consumer. ... But a more efficient collaboration between design and research is necessary. The most impor-tant function of motivation studies may be in aiding control of motivations—to use the discoveries of motivation research to promote acceptance of a product when the principles and sentiments have been developed by the designer. Industry needs greater control of the consumer—a capitalist society needs this as much as a Marx-ist society. The emphasis of the last 10 years on giving the consumer what he thinks he wants is a ludicrous exaggeration of democracy; propaganda techniques could be exploited more systematically by industry to mould the consumer to its own needs. ...

It will take longer to breed desire for possession when the objects to be possessed have sprung not directly from the subconscious of the consumer himself, but from the creative consciousness of an artistic sensibility—but the time lag will have dis-tinct advantages for industry.

An industry programmed five years and more ahead of production has to think big and far-out. Product design, probing into future and unknown markets, must be venturesome and, to be certain of success, stylistically and technically valid. ... New products need market preparation to close the gap. Industry, and with it the design-er, will have to rely increasingly on the media which modify the mass audience—the publicists who not only understand public motivations but who play a large part in directing public response to images. They should be the designers' closest allies, perhaps more important in the team than researchers or sales managers. Ad man, copy-writer and feature editor need to be working together with the designer at the initiation of a programme instead of as a separated group with the task of finding the market for a completed product. The time lag can be used to design a consumer to the product and he can be "manufactured" during the production span. Then producers should not feel inhibited, need not be disturbed by doubts about the re-ception their products may have by an audience they do not trust, the consumer can come from the same drawing board. (Hamilton 1960, 32)

What is perhaps most disturbing about this view is how it illustrates what happens as we push the established idea of "fit" just a little further and more explicitly embrace the idea that the user is some *thing* we design. We might try to defend ourselves by saying that when it comes to design as revision or redesign, this is not so problematic: taking on an existing design and how to improve it, we can study present use and what aspects of the existing design seem to be causing problems. But the question remains: can we really completely separate the domain of correcting mistakes to optimize the fit of an existing thing from the situation when we are venturing out into something new?

Importantly, this is not to say that an emphatic, rich, and reflective understanding of people and practices is not necessary in design. On the contrary, it is fundamental. Rather, this is about what our concepts do for (and to) us, and more generally why, in the words of Bruno Latour, "what the Moderns called 'their future' has never been contemplated face to face, since it has always been the future of someone fleeing their past looking *backward*, not *forward*" (Latour 2010,486). It is about why some things have not changed since the early days of design research as we now know it. Consider Jones's reflection made some four decades ago as he compiled his collection of design methods:

This question of the instability of the present, under the influence of technological changes planned in the past, and coming about in the future, is perhaps the hardest thing to get used to. It is still difficult to accept the, by now, rational view that the investigation of existing needs is not necessarily any guide to what people will want to do when new technical possibilities become available. Of what use, to Henry Ford, would have been a market survey of the pre-1914 demand for private cars and of what use, to the people who are now trying to solve the traffic congestion problem, is a measurement of the existing need for traffic automation?

A great many people will have to lose their belief in the stability of the present before it becomes socially feasible to plan on the basis of what will be possible in the future rather than on the basis of what was possible in the recent past. (Jones 1992, 33)

An Unstable Definition

In the third chapter, I introduced the notion of making a definition through a design. Using a chair as an example, I argued that giving it form in a certain sense also is a matter of making a definition of what "sitting" is. We can say that as we design something, like a chair, we design both a thing and its use. Thus I will introduce a distinction between thing-design and use-design, "thing" in our example being the chair as a physical thing, and "use" referring to the act(s) of sitting. This distinction is different from the one between form and function: whereas both "form" and "function" refer to what an object is and does, "use" refers to what *we* do with it.

Since we need to be more specific about what "use" actually refers to, let us unpack how use becomes defined. If we start with the distinction typically made between designing and using, we can say there are *acts defining use through design* and *acts of defining use through use*. To define use through design is what I do when I design my chair around a particular idea about sitting. "Sitting" could be a general act, but also something quite specific: it could, for instance, be that I want to reduce the risk of health issues at work by designing for a more ergonomic way of sitting, or that I design for a certain context with specific requirements related to sitting, such as the driver's seat of a RIB rescue boat making 60 knots in open waters. It can, of course, also be about a more general understanding of what sitting is, as when designing a sofa for a living room meant to support many different kinds of sitting (some of those acts probably more adequately categorized as acts of sleeping).

Now, to define use through use is what *we* do when we *make use* of the thing. This may or may not include the acts of use intended by the designer. For instance, we may disagree with the ergonomic posture intended and instead decide to sit on the chair in a different way; or we may decide that the best possible use of the chair is to fuel a fire. Indeed, while "defining" the chair as fuel through the act of burning it may seem far-fetched, it actually happens to most chairs at some point: when we no longer want the chair, we throw it away, and it either ends up in a landfill or is burned in some facility. This illustrates another issue arising from not understanding the significant difference between intended and actual use: since we think of use only in terms of intended use, we do not design for use to significantly change during the object's life span, nor do we think about use falling outside our own design intent. As a result, most objects are never really prepared for any other kind of reappropriation or recycling than more basic forms of material separation or energy production such as burning.

The distinctions can be used to articulate a range of different relations between design and use, different ways in which someone can be or become a user. In design approaches oriented toward optimal fit, the purpose is to minimize the influence of acts of defining use through use outside what is included in the set of intended acts of use. This might be central in certain areas, such as safety: in an emergency system used only under intense stress, the space for interpretation and exploration must be minimal to ensure effective and error-free operation. Thus design methodology for such situations needs to work with ways of making actual and intended use as identical as possible. Historically, ways of designing that stem from human factors, such as usability engineering and human-computer interaction, have their origin in safety, aviation, operation of industrial machines, military applications, and so on, and it is therefore not surprising that such methods have a basic orientation toward optimal fit even though their present-day applications may be different.

At the other end of the spectrum, we find approaches intended to empower definitions of use through use, including various forms of "open" design. Consider Cameron Tonkinwise's argument for a kind of "unfinished" design that better meets the challenges of sustainability:

What is at issue is not whether designers are capable of designing nothings rather than things, that is to say, services rather than products, but rather whether designers are capable of designing things that are not finished. It is less a matter of designing a different sort of thing than a matter of a thoroughly different form of designing, one that is perhaps better described as form of "continuous design" or "redesigning." (Tonkinwise 2005, 28)

To generalize, we may say the different relations between how acts of design and acts of use come to define "use" open up a spectrum ranging from trying to simulate *"use" before use* to trying to extend the design process into what we otherwise typically consider to be use, what we may think of as *"design" after design* (Redström 2008).

At one end of the spectrum, we find classical user-centered design, where we use iterative prototyping and user evaluations during a design process to try to find out if actual use will match intended use—what we may call a *"use" before use* approach. At the other end, we find approaches that explore how the specifics of use can be indeterminate and left open for interpretation, as in notions such as "unfinished things" (Tonkinwise 2005), "tactical formlessness" (Hunt 2003), "pure design" (Jones 1992), or "thinging" (Telier et al. 2011)—approaches oriented toward *"design" after design*.

Again, we are still looking at only a part of a spectrum here. When a designer defines the use of something through a given design, it is of course not only the people who will eventually use the thing who become "defined" through the process. For instance, if the thing designed is something to be mass-produced in a factory, many people will in various ways become defined as parts of its production (indeed, even the people designing the thing might be defined on the basis of what is being produced, *what* they make rather than *who* they are [cf. Karlsson and Redström 2015]; most designer roles are named after what parts they produce: graphic designer, interaction designer, textile designer, etc.). Or if the thing created is a service that is continuously performed rather produced only once, the people performing its functions will be correspondingly continuously defined by the design (as in the scripts defining how workers at a call center have to speak, as in the roles expressed through the different uniforms in a restaurant, etc.). Here I have focused on issues located at the center of what we already speak about when doing user-centered design, but there is much more to such acts of defining use through design than this.

The distinction between different acts of defining use, through design and through use respectively, does not offer a new definition of user per se. Rather, it reconfigures the question by seeking an alternative based not on *who* makes such definitions but on *how* they are made. This alternative—to work with a combination of acts defining use through design and through use respectively—is unstable in the sense that while it precisely states how use is defined, it is also indeterminate and fluid until the point where we explicitly state, or eventually find out, what these acts are.

We can respond to this uncertainty by trying to reduce the potential influence of acts redefining use unfolding over time. We can also respond to this inherent uncertainty by acknowledging that some redefinitions of use outside the scope of what can be considered during the design process most likely will happen, and we therefore may need to prepare for them. This can be radical, but it does not have to be: sometimes even the most basic considerations, like making sure that a thing can be taken apart and its materials reused for something else, can make a significant difference compared to when no other forms of use are even considered.

This was one interpretation of why we say that we *make use* of things.

Making a Definition

In this chapter, I have looked into definitions of form and user to see if the idea of making definitions through design could apply also to more general and complex terms. I have argued that even more analytical concepts meant to remain stable over time are defined not only through words but importantly also through specific acts in and of design. The way form is

defined through certain acts of appreciating it, such as images in magazines and exhibitions at museums, seems at least as powerful as any written
account of what form is—also in the context of design history. Looking
into how such definitions work, we could see that, in the case of both form
and user, there were significant issues associated with confusing analytical
terms for projective notions, and that achieving precision through stability
tends to increase the risk for fossilization.

Based on such observations, I suggested alternative definitions of form
and user. Instead of trying to capture the essence of what is form or what
is a user, these alternatives were based on what people do: what the *making*
of such definitions might be like. In the case of form, I worked with the
interplay between expressions and acts of appreciation; in the case of use, I
worked with the interplay between acts of defining use through design and
acts of defining use through use. The result was a kind of definition that is
inherently unstable or *transitional*. If the typical analytical definition has
the structural character of an answer, these notions have a structure more
similar to a question, something that calls for a response.

One might object that these alternative definitions, therefore, are not at
all precise, and this indeterminate fluidity is something that proper theory
would have to remove. But it is precisely this issue that is at stake here:
whether design can actually rely on the same kind of precision that we
come to expect from science, or if it needs something else to support its
development. That there is a basic difference between what already exists
and what might become is quite clear. The question is what this means for
how we conceive of design theory. The transitional theories presented in
this book are meant as a probe into this issue: provided with an alternative,
we can start asking questions about their respective properties in relation to
what we need our theories to do for us.

5 Programs

After discussing in the previous chapter how more complex concepts can be both sustained and unpacked through definitions made through design, let us now return to the spectrum outlined earlier and look into another way of making complex definitions. In chapter 3, I argued that one of the ways that we handle complexity, such as the tensions between the particular and the universal, is to use conceptual spectra populated with more fluid notions that allow us to move along an (imaginary) axis. To address the question of what it means to fundamentally redefine design, I used such a spectrum ranging from what *a* design is to what design*ing* is. Importantly, this spectrum is not about the distinction between design as a thing versus design as an activity, but rather about the continuity between a distinct outcome and the overall effort producing such outcomes. Further, I aimed to show that there are reasons for thinking about terms such as *product*, *project*, and *practice* in terms of where they sit in such a continuous spectrum, and they need to be understood in terms of how they relate to each other through difference rather than each being identified by its individual meaning. Further, I argued that such conceptual precision based on difference rather than static criteria might be central to how these terms support development by being inherently fluid and unstable, an idea further elaborated in chapter 4.

In the middle of this spectrum, between project and practice, I placed the notion of program. In what follows, I first discuss what a program is in more general terms, and why this part of the spectrum might be of special interest to us. I then develop a more specific account of programs in design research and discuss what this kind of "definition made through design" can do for us. Let me, however, start with an anecdote.

Anecdotal Evidence

In 2001, during the process of finishing my PhD thesis, I was struggling
to articulate the basic logic of my inquiry. While there is always the possibility of, basically, rephrasing any (design) proposition as a (design) question,[1] to frame the work using such "research questions" would not have
produced the kind of structural transparency I was looking for. Indeed,
the entire idea of framing the inquiry using dichotomies such as question-
answer, problem-solution, and so on, seemed to suggest a process of
searching, zooming in, and optimizing that was not present in the actual
work. Oriented more toward problem finding than problem solving, the
work was speculative, with the intention of looking for alternatives to
existing design ideals and principles in the rapidly growing area of interaction design. As such it was meant to be critical and projective, intended
to shed light on what was seemingly taken for granted by presenting
alternatives, by suggesting that things could be different. To exemplify,
we were proposing design approaches such as "slow technology" as an
alternative to then-dominant ideas about usability and efficiency as the
primary objectives of technology development and design (Hallnäs and
Redström 2001).

We had already worked with notions of design programs (such as slow
technology), and with much help and support from Lars Hallnäs, what
came out of these discussions and doubts was the following:

The research process begins with formulating a design program based on a set of
initial conjectures about the design space and how to investigate it. The investigation undertaken in this thesis is not about refining and optimising existing artefacts,
but rather on the development of a collection of examples that illustrate different
possibilities within this design space. Thus, this is not a well-defined problem that
lends itself to a rationalistic search for an optimal solution. Instead, we use experimental design as a way of finding a path into a problem that is poorly understood
at the outset. A design program serves as a starting point and a framework for such
investigation.

The next step is to formulate more specific design ideas and working hypotheses
that can be addressed in practical work, i.e., by working with designing, implementing, testing and evaluating prototypes. In all of these steps, new experiences
are gained and new design opportunities are discovered; the implementation of a
specific prototype can expose new design opportunities, as can results from a field
study of some specific situation or setting. Of central importance is to be attentive
to what happens during this process of realising the ideas from the design program,

since just working through the steps to arrive at a final solution will not in itself result in the knowledge we are after. The experience gained and the new design opportunities discovered lead to a new set of working hypotheses, usually directed towards a more specific part of the design space, and finally to reformulation of the design program or the development of a new design program. Thus, we have a process of:

i)   formulating a design program;
ii) realising the program by designing, implementing and evaluating design examples;
iii) reflection and formulation of results, e.g., reporting on the experiences gained, formulating new working hypotheses, reformulating the design program.

This process is in part similar to methods for iterative prototyping and stepwise refinement in systems development, where one moves from the more abstract towards the more concrete in iterative steps. An important difference, however, is that the method employed here is not primarily designed to lead to increasingly more advanced or "better" prototypes. Instead, it is the development of the questions asked and the hypotheses posed that are in focus: we move from the more general to the more specific as our understanding of the design space deepens and we are able to formulate new and more detailed hypotheses. Thus, the prototypes themselves are not necessarily more advanced in later steps of this process, which in turn is one reason for referring to them as design examples instead. (Redström 2001, 26)

This became the starting point of a longer exploration of the potential of using programs to try to make sense of, and articulate how, such experimental design research works. Other related and more recent accounts capture different aspects of this process,[2] but given the general idea of examining the way we do design theory, I want to start with this one to show its openings as well as its misconceptions.

Programs

The term "program" is used in a range of diverse settings, among them computer software, television shows, educational curricula, frameworks for scientific inquiry, and architectural planning of space. Such different programs may not share many similarities, but they have at least one common feature: they are about the intent and structure behind something about to unfold. A program can be a planned set of events or actions, as when we talk about the program of an art or a music festival; it can be the overall intention and planning governing the development of a new technology, infrastructure, or sector, as in a nation's nuclear program or the different programs run by the United Nations;[3] it can be the planning of (public) space to serve one or many, sometimes even contradictory, purposes (e.g., Tschumi 1996).

In academia, two kinds of programs stand out: educational programs and research programs. Educational programs are specific compositions of courses and content, often with a particular academic degree as the primary intended outcome. Indeed, the specificity of the composition is crucial to understanding what makes an educational program into what it is, and even within a fairly defined subject there are significant differences across programs depending on the priorities made, the expertise at the institution offering the education, and so on. To understand someone's educational profile, we typically ask not only what she studied but also where and with what program.

An educational program also illustrates that what actually constitutes a program as performed is much more than its ideas and intentions. What makes a program into what it is, is also an assemblage of material resources, institutional contexts, infrastructures, economic conditions, and so on, and not the least something brought together and made by people (also bringing in, presumably, different experiences, ideas, agendas, objectives, etc.). Keeping in mind that we are addressing complex "material-discursive practices" (Barad 2007), however, I will still try to follow the trajectory of the previous chapters and focus on what we may call the conceptual structures of programs.

Research programs can be frameworks for funding schemes, but they may also be articulations of larger research efforts. A specific meaning of the term "research programme" (often spelled "programme" to differentiate it from programs in general—a convention that I follow here) was offered by Imre Lakatos (e.g., Lakatos and Feyerabend 1999). Lakatos's notion was partly a response to Thomas Kuhn's notion of "paradigm" and describes the overall framework that science operates within, something akin to a worldview, a set of theories held true as a foundation for further research. Thus while there can be research programs in the sense of research efforts of a certain scope and scale (such as the research programs built around, say, a particle accelerator facility like CERN),[4] then a programme in this sense would correspond to the overall scientific framework within which the more specific effort is carried out (such as particle physics). With respect to the spectrum outlined in chapter 3, Lakatos's notion of programme is therefore located at the "general" end, beyond the point where I placed "paradigm" (as I used it in the more, by now, everyday and much less specific sense of the term compared to what Kuhn originally intended).

Although addressing something quite different from what is at stake in my inquiry, Lakatos's account of programmes contains some ideas about the structure and unfolding of research that are also relevant here. Lakatos's defense of certain ideas about rationality in science originating in the work of Karl Popper is perhaps less relevant to contemporary design, but some of the ideas about principles for what makes a research programme progressive (or degenerative) could shed light also on how design develops. With respect to the discussion about form in the previous chapter, for instance, it is interesting to note how he argues that a programme maintains a "hard core" of basic assumptions or theories that are never really questioned. Indeed, accepting the hard core is necessary for participating in the programme. Development over time, therefore, primarily happens in the "protective belt" surrounding the hard core, and as long as this development continuously leads to new ideas, new theories, and so on, the programme remains progressive. However, when developments in the protective belt end up being only about protecting the hard core from being challenged by alternative theories and predictions, new observations not accounted for, and so on, then the programme begins to degenerate. This is just one of many images of how science works, and a contested one at that—but in terms of unpacking notions of programs, it has its merits.

The combination of intent and unfolding that seems to be one of the few shared characteristics of the many different kinds of programs we may encounter is intriguing, as it seems so closely related to what designing is about. To understand the term's usefulness for the present inquiry into design theory, however, we also need to look at the difference between program and project. As outlined in chapter 3, the difference between the two seems to be one of continuous nuance rather than discrete kind, and if we look at development over time, it is not hard to find examples of how a project starts to drift toward becoming a program as it gains traction and increases its resources and influence—for example, consider how we refer to "the Manhattan Project" but later talk of "nuclear programs." Thus a potential *difference* to build on when understanding the difference between project and program would be scale and scope.

A more interesting place to look for such a difference, however, would be to pick up on Lakatos's idea that what characterizes a research programme is that it contains a hard core of theories and beliefs that are held to be true. This would allow us to articulate a difference with respect to influence that is not quantitative but qualitative: it is not a difference in the amount of resources we are talking about. For a programme to work, its hard core must not be questioned or tampered with. Thus one suggestion would be that while a project may be open or closed with respect to various issues, a program more fundamentally depends on a certain worldview—a certain set of theories, beliefs, articulations, assumptions, and so on—to do its thing. I will unpack this idea further later, but just to see some of its contours, consider an educational program, its courses, learning objectives, outcomes, and so on. Now, how much of this can change as part of continuous development efforts in projects and courses—and what (kinds of) changes require a reformulation of the program as such? Indeed, considering the notion of a "protective belt," can we think of instances where such continuous adjustments actually begin to serve the purpose of protecting the hard core from being questioned?

In what follows, I elaborate on a more particular notion of programs in design. A few observations about programs in general from this brief overview will form part of the discussion's basis:

• A program is characterized by both intent and unfolding, an intertwining of projection and process.
• A program depends on a certain worldview, a basic set of beliefs and assumptions, to be effective.
• A program's development is not indefinitely continuous but must come to an end when its worldview is fundamentally questioned.

To these points we may add what could be seen in the spectrum of definitions of design made through making: the idea that programs sit somewhere in the middle of the tension between the particular and the general, and thus in the area perhaps most exposed to the difficulties of this dichotomy.

As in the previous chapter, I first look into what happens when we keep foundations static at the level of "provisional worldviews." I then develop a notion of design research programs to articulate another approach along the lines of seeking more unstable and transitional alternatives.

Tipping Point

In science we talk about "basic research," research that is not governed by an interest in a particular application or more practical outcome but aims at the very foundations of the domain in question. Design,[5] on the other hand, is inherently about making, about the particular, as something acting in the service of others.[6] It has been called an "applied art," and thus the existence of a corresponding "basic research" in design could be doubted or even completely rejected. As the term "applied art" suggests, this issue was once resolved by considering design to rest on an artistic foundation. In the early history of (industrial) design education in schools like the Bauhaus, the relation to such artistic foundations was straightforward: students were partially trained *as* artists *by* artists. It is easy to see the relation between design and its artistic foundations in teaching materials such as Vasilij Kandinsky's *Point and Line to Plane* or Paul Klee's notebooks from the time he taught at the Bauhaus.[7]

Over time, these artistic foundations have expanded, but as my earlier discussion of form showed, they have not been able to cope with the development happening in design practice. Already at HfG Ulm, still so close to the Bauhaus that Walter Gropius was part of its inauguration, we could see beginning struggles with artistic foundations and design as a matter of their "application": "Is design an applied art, in which case it is to be found in the elements of the square, the triangle, and the circle; or is it a discipline that draws its criteria from the tasks it has to perform, from use, from making, and from technology?" Otl Aicher asked (1991, 126).

And so let us look at what happens when we pursue design research in this way, keeping with the idea that what we do is a matter of "application" and that our foundations are provided by more basic research happening in other areas. The story might go something like this:

To start, we say that our primary concern is design practice (in the wide sense of the word practice). We talk about research through design, practice-based research, and so on (fig. 5.1).

Practice

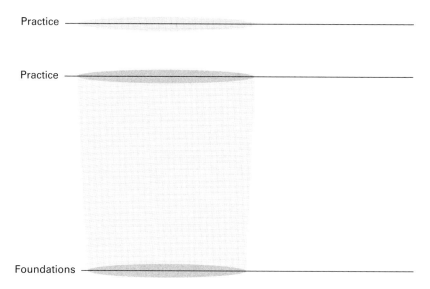

Practice

Foundations

Figures 5.1–5.2

But we also say that this practice rests on an artistic foundation. Indeed, this is not just something we say: in countries such as mine, Sweden, it is also a matter of how the legislation governing higher education distinguishes between education conducted on a scientific or an artistic foundation (fig. 5.2).

While it is clear that design practice and artistic foundation are two different things, there is a rather direct correspondence. If we consider form, for instance, we could think about such relations as giving form to everyday objects, on the one hand, and a foundational artistic understanding of visual expressions, composition, proportions, shape and volume, and so on, on the other. We teach such correspondence in classes such as visualization, sketching and drawing, model making, and so forth.

Now, what happens over time is that design practice expands into new domains: addressing new issues and design problems, developing at the intersections with other areas and disciplines by borrowing concepts and methods. Thus we get something like what we see in figure 5.3.

And as design never stops interacting, continuously bringing new ideas and influences inside of it and expanding into new territories, this tendency continues over time, as shown in figures 5.4 and 5.5.

This expansion is in itself not problematic; on the contrary, it is very much a matter of design being alive and evolving. What *is* problematic is that the foundations are not developing nearly as much, and certainly not in the same way as our practices.[8]

Over time, this tension is becoming increasingly pressing. But we move on, adding new design practices to our family as we respond to emerging needs and opportunities (*product* design, *interaction* design, *service* design, *experience* design, *sustainable* design, *social* design, etc.). Still maintaining the idea that what we do rests on an artistic foundation, we eventually get to a point where it becomes difficult to explain how these foundations actually support practice. By now, we are used to this, but we still encounter its effects, as when trying to explain why people who seemingly have their disciplinary foundation in the visualization and materialization of prototypes intended for mass production are also the ones to lead and structure social innovation, rethink health care, address the effects of massive urbanization, or redirect everyday routines toward a more sustainable development.

Then, as so many other times when in doubt, we instead turn to methods and process to articulate and explain what we do—as if that would somehow make the issue of conceptual foundations disappear. And so, not surprisingly, and despite the dramatic changes in scope, impact, role, and objectives, the design community keeps celebrating pure design form in the same ways that it has done for a century, in exhibitions, magazines, and other such venues—much as its siblings born out of engineering contexts continue to celebrate the marvels of new technology in trade fairs, conferences, and more.

This story about design and its development may or may not be correct, and it is anyway a horrid oversimplification. On top of being a caricature, it does not account for what happens if we actually extend or even reject existing foundations before we reach a tipping point, and instead form new practice on new foundations—and there are, of course, many examples of people, studios, and educational programs that have set out to do precisely this (sometimes successfully so, but at times also suffering the consequences of pushing the boundaries of existing institutional frameworks and disciplinary criteria for funding and accreditation). Further, this narrative does not account for the possibilities of instead turning to inter- or

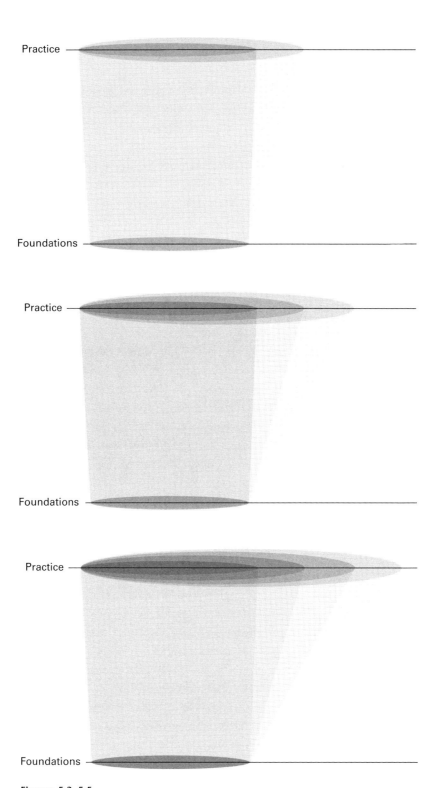

Figures 5.3–5.5

transdisciplinary perspectives, rethinking what the relation between practice and foundations can be like. Thus there is a range of alternatives if we want one.

However, if for the time being we stay with what is already established, and why we feel inclined to at least sometimes think of design in terms of "discipline," there are at least two main reasons for looking at a story like this. The first is that if we reject the primary foundations of our domain and instead aim for another one, it is also likely that what we do will not be understood as being about the same thing. Arguing against design as discipline, Klaus Krippendorff remarks that thinking about design in such terms "would invite designers to police each other for whether they qualify to be called designers, perhaps until they have succeeded to internalize the norms of their discipline and show evidence of having enough self-discipline to police themselves" (Krippendorff 2016, 197). Indeed, while we might want to think otherwise, this is likely the actual condition. To use Michel Foucault's (1977) terms, it is difficult to see how the examinations happening in design and design research would somehow be inherently different from all other rituals of examination. Power is exercised through disciplining, and if we want to be in dialogue with a particular domain, we somehow need to relate to this. To exemplify: you cannot be admitted to an educational program without making an application, which will be *reviewed* and ranked; you cannot present your work at a conference without submitting a paper, which will be *reviewed* and ranked; you cannot get a position in a department without making an application, which will be *reviewed* and ranked; and so on and so forth. In all these processes of selecting among options, there is an element of examination in which what we believe to be the foundation of our domain plays its part. Thus, in relation to Lakatos's account, if the critique we aim to offer does not explicitly acknowledge the basic beliefs of the programme's hard core, then the programme's protective belt will make sure that such critique has no effect whatsoever on how it develops.

Whether we support the notion of design as discipline or not, we therefore still need to acknowledge certain disciplinary characteristics if we are to understand the *stabilizing* structures of design and designing. To use a historical example, consider John Chris Jones's reflections on, and reactions against, the design methods movement he was initially part of, and the tension between looking for a different foundation and orientation, on the one hand, and at the same time still wanting to speak to what is established as "designing":

Looking back now, at this book, and at what has become of design methods, I think that this is the crux of the matter: the new methods *permit* collaborative designing whereas the old methods do *not*. They change the nature of designing, or can if one lets them. The essential point is that the new methods permit collaboration *before* "the concept," the organising idea, the back-of-the-envelope-sketch, "the design" as emerged (providing the leading designer knows how to switch from being the person responsible for the result to being the one who ensures that "the process is right"). (Jones 1992, xxxiii)

What are the blocks of collaborative design? What stops us from acting together as a context for our works, adapting freely to what we discover in doing what we do? The blocks are product-thinking, function-fixing, role-fixing, cost-reducing, and our identification of ourselves with these things instead of with our thoughts, feelings, minds, common-sense awareness of what is needed but what we're not paid to do. All of this leaves us over-adapted to the status quo (which we identify with self, with security, when in fact it's what destroys the self, the being, the joy of living). ... The first practical step to unblocking, to being free to be inventive, and collaborative, is to widen, and to overlap, our job specifications, our roles. Once that happens the whole context begins to become mobile. (Jones 1984, 214)

The essential first step is to accept the roughness, the unprofessional character, the reaction "that's not design, anyone can do it" of improvised initiatives by users themselves, by us as we are as persons, unspecialised. (Jones 1984, 206)

The second reason why it is important to consider this story from a kind of disciplining "inside" is that it also points to what issues this research addresses and what issues it leaves aside. Indeed, the story does not have to be true for us to see a basic problem with design research primarily committed to practice and applications without much attention to the poetics and politics of its foundations. While design research based on the perspective of the external observer analyzing what exists is problematic because of the stable and static conceptions it tends to favor, design research driven by practice might also not succeed in providing what we need to develop: if it leaves its (artistic or other) foundations untouched, the resulting trajectory is awkwardly similar to a tipping trash can. To use Lakatos's terms, research that never commits to critiquing its foundational elements would—for structural reasons—be a kind of research that significantly risks never being able to challenge and develop its own hard core.[9]

Fortunately, being about the *artificial*—what is made rather than given—means that design is never out of options, as there will always be alternatives. In what follows, I argue that programs offer one such alternative way of approaching these issues.

Design Research Programs

From the brief introduction of programs, it seems that research efforts located in this part of the spectrum depend on a set of basic assumptions or beliefs: they carry with them a certain worldview. At the same time, however, we can also see that keeping such foundations static is problematic, especially if they are also kept out of the reach of what the research efforts in question actually engage with. Thus we want to look for support structures that somehow cater to the need of a worldview, a hard core, but do so in a more nonprotective way. This could, for instance, happen by making sure there are always competing worldviews advocated by other such support structures, and we make sure that the activities that unfold within our structure constantly challenge this worldview, searching for its breaking points rather than its comfort zones. That would allow us to work at a level of generality that engages with worldviews but does so in a more open and critical rather than affirmative and protective way. I will argue that design research programs can be set up to do precisely this: to enable us to work with a diverse set of inherently unstable and transitional worldviews.

Figure 5.6
A design research program.

Let us start with a simple image of what this could look like. In its most basic form, the programmatic design research structure consists of two elements:

- Program: a set of basic beliefs, design ideals, intentions, etc.
- Experiments: a set of design experiments expressing the program.

For example, consider a program based on the following statement: "Design is the use of the basic geometrical shapes of the circle, the square, and the triangle to express the functionality of everyday things." Through design experiments, we would then explore what *designing* would be like according to this program through the (re)design of various everyday objects. To find out what the design space of this program is like, our experiments would probably initially explore issues such as how objects with more complex forms could be reduced to these elementary geometrical compositions. In a sense, we would look for what are *typical*, as in the notion of the "prototype" (Moholy-Nagy 1998), examples of what this kind of designing is like.

After a series of such experiments, we will have come to know quite well the central positions of the design space created by this program; and thus to learn new things and avoid mere repetition, we will start pushing the experiments in other directions, now turning toward the edges and extremes. For instance, we might set off in the direction of designing for the human body, exploring the interactions between strict geometry and ergonomics. Or we might start asking questions about what kinds of artistic expression are possible within the frames of the program, and what "functionality" really refers to. We begin to understand what kind of design the program makes possible and what falls outside it—and we come to a point where we either stay with this worldview or decide that it is now exhausted (from a learning point of view, with respect to research, artistic expression, or whatever reason we had for once starting to work with it), and it therefore is time to end it.[10]

Now, to what extent is this an expression of a worldview? First, "worldview" here is understood as a set of basic beliefs or assumptions that constitute the "world" for the design, in the sense that they are not really questioned or challenged but rather assumed as its basic condition. We are not speaking of worldview in the sense of a complete human experience; on the contrary, for this to work, it is central that we can find ourselves both inside and outside the program, although our design work is conditioned by it. Second, the program is a very simplistic and limited one, so its world will be equally limited.

Still, there are things we can say about its basic beliefs, such as that it brings forth a definition of form that is inherently visual and even geometrically reductive, that it understands purpose primarily as functionality, and that it believes the domain of design to be the expressions of everyday things. To understand its world, we can also look at what is clearly not present in its projection, such as for whom the design is made; for what reasons the functionality of the object is in focus, and not what people use it for; that it says nothing about how to prioritize use and management of resources in a global context; and so on. So while this is an extremely limited set of assumptions, the resulting worldview certainly has real implications, in a larger context potentially both productive and destructive ones. And though this worldview is limited and constrained, this makes it clear that it is *situated*: insisting that it must be understood as something particular, as something representing a position.[11]

As we step out of the program, we also leave the worldview it prompted us to accept. While working within the program, exploring what designing is according to its worldview, we had to take it for granted. Now that we leave it, looking at it alongside other such programs, we can see what its definition of what designing is means and what it leads to. Indeed, we can invite other perspectives based on analysis of the existing in the evaluation: because we are no longer talking about projections into potentials but dealing with actual "definitions through design"—as material as a real chair that one can sit in—a necessary basis for discussion has been established (if we have done our job with the program properly, that is). Thus, from the inside, the design program is a call for action: "This *is* what designing is!" From the outside, the design program allows us to ask questions: "Designing *could be* this; what would be its implications?"

In this way, we can use programs to articulate provisional foundations, to state worldviews that we want to explore *as if* they were true so as to learn something about what kind of design they would lead to.[12] Now, if this is the general idea about programmatic design research, then there is clearly a range of issues we need to address to understand how this works.

Provisional and Unstable

While I suggested that programs may offer a possibility of working with transitional rather than static foundations, programs also have the potential to develop into stable structures. Indeed, it is easy to think that what makes a program "successful" is that it develops ever more stable foundations as it increases in scope, resources, and commitment over time. It is likely that we might think that these programs would ideally follow a development curve similar to the large-scale scientific programmes that Lakatos addressed.[13] What I would argue, however, is that there are reasons for resisting such tendencies and instead conceiving of the program as an opportunity to experiment with intentionally transitional foundations for design.

From my earlier story about the risk of tipping points, we learn that design research in general, and research through design in particular, needs to pay attention to how it builds on its foundations, artistic or otherwise. Whether such foundational notions are imported from another discipline or developed "in-house," certain basic questions about what set of basic beliefs that the design work builds on still have to be addressed. Now, in our spectrum of different kinds of definitions made through design, the first time that the issue of basic beliefs turns up is when we come to programs. While our worldviews certainly shine through in both products and projects, with programs they come to the foreground. Thus an informed guess would be that programs represent the minimal kind of definitions made through design that allow us to systematically explore issues related to having a hard core, a set of assumptions that are not to be tampered with. In other words, rather than thinking of programs as a step toward stable foundations, we could consider them a primary experimental ground for exploring the implications of various basic beliefs, of various worldviews. Doing so, however, calls for a slightly different approach to their articulation.

Since a continuously expanding scope is necessary to ensure that research develops new areas and ideas, a first constraint would be restrictions with respect to scope. A program that allows anything to happen will not work; a program that aims to be inclusive in the sense of allowing (too) many different design directions will not be particularly effective. Consider, for instance, making the following addition to the example program sketched earlier: "Design is the use of the basic geometrical shapes of the circle, the square, and the triangle *or any other form* to express the functionality of everyday things." This new program would certainly be able to include much more, but it does not at all call for action in the same way as the original one did. On the contrary, it looks more like a somewhat unfortunate general definition of what much product design used to be about. Thus a fine balance is involved in creating something with both a suggestive openness and inherent limitations.

It is also crucial that we treat the program as provisional and not try to stabilize it. Following Lakatos's notion of a protective belt around a hard core, we can easily end up with work that explores new ideas and directions but only does so in ways that never really challenge the basic ideas behind the program. To reduce the risk of only producing more or less typical experiments, we need to seek the program's boundaries and breaking points, to push ourselves out of its comfort zones.

An additional yet very important cause of instability is the existence of other programs, the simultaneous existence of many alternative worldviews. Unlike science, where unified theory is a legitimate objective, design is about the possible, about how things could be. If we do not subscribe to deep determinism, we have little reason to direct our attention to just one out of many design futures. In a strict sense, design is never necessary but always contingent: had we made our design decisions differently, then things would be different. When a designer says, about a given form of expression, for instance, that it is *necessary*, it means that for the design to be consistent, this is, in his or her view, the only possible way to do it. While part of such understood and interpreted necessities might have to with laws of physics (such as what is possible to do with a given material, that gravity still matters, etc.), this understanding of "necessary" is quite different from the notion of necessity that Sir Isaac Newton had in mind. As much as we want to formulate principles of aesthetics along lines similar to laws of motion, we can never cross the divide between necessary and contingent or overcome the difference between theorizing what exists and expressing what may become. Even in our imaginary program aiming for ideal geometrical form, no matter how *idealistic* our ambitions might be, we will still make circles, not Circle; squares, not Square; and triangles, not Triangle.

This interest in the particularities of design programs makes the framework presented here inherently different from Lakatos's account, as he is

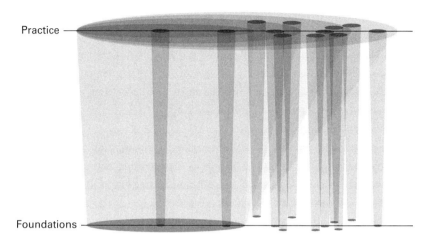

Figure 5.7
Many design research programs.

searching for an overall rationality regarding the foundations and progress of science per se. In contrast, the definition of what design is that is made through a given program will always be contested by the presence of other such worldviews, and instead of ending up in meaningless and continuously unproductive disagreements about what a general definition of what "design," "user," "form," or some other basic concept should be like, we can work with a multitude of such definitions *made* through different programs and their associated experiments.

In other words, this is a way to try to explain how and why the parallel existence of different and sometimes conflicting foundations is not problematic but rather an effective response to the dangers of unified theory in a context where contingencies rather than necessities dominate, and where the potential rather than the actual is the objective. Intriguingly, design is somewhat like history in this sense: since every story is told by someone somewhere, only through different accounts will we be able to grasp the bigger picture, its poetics *and* politics. Similarly, we need to ask questions about *whose* design we are dealing with. As Clive Dilnot describes the condition of design: "That the artificial is therefore, in strict terms, beyond law and beyond certainty means that the propositional is *structurally inherent* to the artificial. This means in turn that the artificial is a world of the possible, *not* as extrapolation, or as subjective will ('I demand!') but as its deepest condition" (Dilnot 2015, 180).

Design research must therefore also include basic research, not in the sense of locating that invariant universal foundation that everything else can depend on, but in the sense of, again and again, asking basic questions about what design is and how it is done. Or else our applied research might as well become just implied research.

Design Experiments

The notion of an experiment is a complex topic and a debate as long as the history of research. Indeed, earlier in history, the notion of experimental method was more or less synonymous with scientific method, and for many, the typical image of a researcher is still a person in a lab coat. But the notion of experimentation holds more than this: experimental art, experimental vehicles, experimental living, and all sorts of activities conducted with the purpose of pushing boundaries and exploring alternatives. The understanding of the design experiment advocated here is rooted in the long history of labeling design that explores boundaries and alternatives as experimental—hence the notion that this is a kind of experimental design research.

In terms of research, however, the ideas presented here also comes with influences from the new experimentalism and revitalization of ideas about relations between theory development and experimentation historically stemming from, for instance, Francis Bacon, and advocated by philosophers of science such as Ian Hacking (1983). Importantly, what is brought forward from this discourse on the philosophy of science is not support for a search for scientific method in design but rather notions of certain structural similarities that may point to important aspects of how experimental design research works. Thus I am concerned here not with the issue of scientific inquiry but with aspects of how making/experimenting and theorizing are intertwined, and how experiments can operate in many different ways and for different purposes (cf. Hall 2011). As Dagmar Steffen concluded in her overview of experimentalism in design research:

It should become apparent that an exclusive appropriation of experimentalism on the part of the scholarly research culture in opposition to creative practices in the arts seems to be untenable. It rather stands to reason that practice-led design research has the potential to following up the experimental practices in Renaissance and to reconcile the "two cultures"—not necessarily science and the arts, but the culture of scholarly discursive knowledge and the presentational symbolism of the arts. (Steffen 2014, 1.14)

Historical accounts tend to enforce the idea that theory precedes making and experimentation, a tendency that has also made its way into design. In his critique of such an ordering, Ian Hacking distinguishes between a weak and a strong version of this argument. The weak version suggests that you only need to have some ideas about nature and your apparatus before you can conduct an experiment. Basically, the experiment needs some kind of direction, or else it is likely to result in a set of observations with little or no meaning (cf. Bang et al. 2012). The strong version, however, says that "your experiment is significant only if you are testing a theory about the phenomena under scrutiny" (Hacking 1983, 154). Hacking offers a range of examples where this is clearly not the case,[14] and there are reasons for rejecting the strong version and also doubting the weak one: "The relationships between theory and experiment differ at different stages of development, nor do all the natural sciences go through the same cycles" (154).

As I argue later, this is true also in the case of the relations between design programs and their experiments; the idea that programs precede experimentation evident in the opening anecdote is simply not correct, and overall the relationship between program and experiment is much more complex and dynamic. Indeed, what is important about the program from a design theory point of view is not that it precedes or governs experimentation but that it constitutes a definition of what designing is at a level of abstraction that experiments as such do not address.

Following this, we can therefore not simply define the design experiment as an act or intervention intended to materialize, explore, or challenge a given design program. That would be similar to subscribing to the strong version of the theory-precedes-experiment argument. Just as often, the trajectory will be pointing in the opposite direction, starting with experiments long before a more general framing has been articulated. Clearly, even within an overall methodological framework built on the idea of programmatic design research, our understanding of the design experiment must also include things happening before the formulation of a program. This leads us to the issue of how we understand and articulate the relation between experiments and programs, and how such relations unfold over time.

Program versus Experiment

As Hacking argued, histories of science have a tendency to order experiments after theory, but closer inspection often reveals that this was not
actually the case. In design, we seem to feel a similar urge, as when we
struggle to formulate a research question to guide and define the purpose
of design experimentation, or as when we for some reason still encourage
students to account for theory first in their theses, even when we know the
work unfolded the other way around.

I have spent quite some time on the formative early days of industrial
design in this book, and so let us look at another example from the Bauhaus
to illustrate this issue. In "Principles of Bauhaus Production" for the new
school in Dessau 1926, Walter Gropius declared:

The Bauhaus wants to serve in the development of present-day housing, from the
simplest household appliances to the finished dwelling. In the conviction that
household appliances and furnishings must be rationally related to each other, the
Bauhaus is seeking—by systematic practical and theoretical research in the formal,
technical and economic fields—to derive the design of an object from its natural
functions and relationship. (Gropius 1970, 95)

From the point of view of a design (research) program, several basic propositions are put forward here, such as the rational order of things, the systematic research that grounds design, and the concern for the entire living
environment of the home (in a sense anticipating what we today call systems or ecologies of things). Such ideas have formed the basis of industrial
design practice ever since, but the question is: Were they there from the
start? Was work at the Bauhaus really that systematic, deriving its designs,
driven by its manifestos?

Looking at accounts of what it was like to be a student at the Bauhaus, it
seems they were not. Anni Albers (1968), a famous textile designer, recalls
the following in an interview:

SEVIM FESCI Yes. Before we leave the Bauhaus, because we were still there—I would
like to ask you what is this creative atmosphere of the Bauhaus?
ANNI ALBERS This is what I mentioned there in the article—well, the Bauhaus today
is thought of always as a school, a very adventurous and interesting one, to which
you went and were taught something; that it was a readymade spirit. But when I got
there in 1922, that wasn't true at all. It was in a great muddle and there was a great
searching going on from all sides. And people like Klee and Kandinsky weren't recognized as the great masters. They were starting to find their way. And this kind of

general searching was very exciting. And in my little articles this is what I called the creative vacuum. But the word "education" was never mentioned. And the people we think of as the great masters—Klee and Kandinsky—they weren't available for questions. They were the great silent ones who talked among themselves maybe, but never to small little students like me. But we knew that what the Academy was doing was wrong and it was exciting that you knew you had the freedom to try out something. And that was fine. But, as I say, it wasn't that you went there and were taking something home from there. You were a contributor.

SEVIM FESCI   It was more a kind of laboratory.

ANNI ALBERS   Yes, from all sides. Everybody tried his best and we didn't know in which direction we were going. Because there was nothing. You only knew that what there was in other schools or academies was wrong and didn't satisfy.

Clearly the basic conditions for experimental design work must have been part of the basic visions of making the Bauhaus happen, but their precise formulation as we now think of them seemed to have emerged over time— not only through manifestos but importantly also through making. Albers comments on these origins:

At the Bauhaus, those beginning to work in textiles at that time, for example, were fortunate not to have had the traditional training in the craft: it is no easy task to throw useless conventions overboard. ...

But how to begin? At first they played with the material quite amateurishly. Gradually, however, something emerged which looked like the beginning of a new style. Technique was picked up as it was found to be needed and insofar as it might serve as a basis for future experimentation.

Unburdened by any considerations of practical application, this uninhibited play with materials resulted in amazing objects, striking in their newness of conception in regard to use of color and compositional elements. (Albers 2000, 3)

A most curious change took place when the idea of a practical purpose, a purpose aside from the purely artistic one, suggested itself to this group of weavers. Such a thought, ordinarily in the foreground, had not occurred to them, having been so deeply absorbed in the problems of the material itself and the discoveries of unlimited ways of handling them. This consideration of usefulness brought about a profoundly different conception. A shift took place from the free play with forms to a logical building of structures. ... Concentrating on a purpose had a disciplining effect, now that the range of possibilities had been freely explored. (4)

Bringing Albers's observations to the issue of how the relations between program and experiments are established and unfold, we can make several remarks. First of all, it is obvious that we would be mistaken to follow the historical tendency to think of the Bauhaus as being built on a manifesto, a programmatic declaration of intent. Certainly it was—but equally from the creation of an environment encouraging experimentation, where new ideas could emerge through making. It probably took quite some time before these two trajectories married and became the Bauhaus as we think of it today.

The second thing to note is what happens to the experimentation once such a programmatic frame starts to emerge, what Albers describes as how "consideration of usefulness brought about a profoundly different conception," and how "concentrating on a purpose had a *disciplining* effect, now that the range of possibilities had been freely explored" (2000, 4; my italics). Revisiting the idea that an experiment is an experiment only if it is meant to address a particular theory (or in our case perhaps that "the experiment expresses the program"), we can say that while the order of things might differ, there is something about how the program offers a particular perspective on the experiment even when the experimentation initially preceded the formation of a program. Thus we might well end up in a situation where an experiment that was conducted long before the given program was articulated can still become an experiment within that program by being brought into it and seen through the lens of the program's worldview.[15]

The Typical Example

The way that program and experiments seem to depend on each other for precision—the research process perhaps beginning with one of them but not really starting before both are in place—is difficult to handle from a methodological point of view. Indeed, although many of the main ingredients are there, the account described in the opening anecdote was clearly mistaken when it comes to many aspects of how they come together.

Throughout this inquiry, I have argued that definitions made through design, through making, play a most central role and need to move to the foreground if we are to see how this kind of research works. Sitting in the middle of a spectrum of definitions spanning from the particular to the general, the design research program makes a kind of definition that is partly about what design*ing* is. This aspect of the program can (primarily) be seen in the worldview it advocates, the set of basic beliefs it asks us to accept as a condition for participating. The experiment, on the other hand, makes a kind of definition that is close to what *a* design is. If we, as part of our work with the imaginary geometrical design program described earlier, create a chair, it would be possible to consider it (like any other chair) to be primarily yet another definition of what sitting is (as discussed in chap. 3). To be interpreted as such, it would not even depend on the existence of a program: the people trying it out may or may not at all care about the existence of such a frame of inquiry.

This means that while the experiment belongs to a program, it has—considered as a definition made through design—also always a certain autonomy. As Ian Hacking put it in the context of science, "Or shall we say that although some theory precedes some experiment, some experiment and some observation precedes theory, and may for long have a life of its own?"(Hacking 1983, 160). This allows experiments to exist on their own, to travel between, to lead the way into—or out of—programs and more.[16] Importantly, this means that definitions made through design experiments also become part of what defines the overall programmatic structure. In other words, this is a matter of an interplay primarily between two different kinds of definitions made through design, and how this mutual dependence unfolds over time.

A key characteristic of this interplay, and a consequence of the partial autonomy of the experiment and its resulting contribution to the whole, can be seen in the frequent existence of *typical* design examples within design programs: experiments that seem to exemplify to the point of almost defining what the program is about. To use historically significant examples, consider, for instance, Dieter Rams's radio for Braun as a *typical* example of the Braun-HfG collaboration; the Carlton bookcase by Ettore Sottsass as a *typical* example of a piece of furniture from Memphis, or the Barcelona Pavilion as a *typical* building by Ludwig Mies van der Rohe (or, indeed, as a *typical* example of modernist architecture)—but consider also a *typical* degree project from an educational program you follow. In chapter 3, I used the example of the Xerox PARC ubiquitous computing experiments to illustrate how an inquiry developed from experiment via project to program (Weiser 1991). This example also illustrates the strong stabilizing or normative effect of certain experiments: not only do their tabs, pads, and boards play an important role in defining what ubiquitous computing became at Xerox PARC, but they have also had a strong influence even on the commercial designs that have followed since.

Perhaps this is what László Moholy-Nagy was pointing to in 1923 when he wrote: "It [The Bauhaus] applies itself to this task in experimental workshops, it designs prototypes for the whole of the house as well as the teapot, and it works to improve our entire way of life by means of economic production which is only possible with the aid of the prototype" (Moholy-Nagy 1998, 303).

And so when we think of the Bauhaus or the HfG Ulm, we more or less simultaneously picture both an idea of what designing is all about and a series of images of what such design appears like. We think of modernism simultaneously as idea *and* image. We do this to the extent that it is truly difficult to envision a given program's designs looking another way, or to think of its design objects as instead typical examples of another program articulated with another purpose—although we know both options ought to be quite *possible*.

What we see here is also a glimpse of another spectrum: one that starts with the *prototype* on one end, and where we find the *stereotype* on the other; the *typical* in the sense discussed earlier is located somewhere in between. Whereas the prototypical retains an inherently propositional character, being something that explicitly exists before, *by definition* an early form that precedes other forms that will follow (and thus in its very character something transitional), the stereotypical is an expression of stability, "of repetition without variation."[17] Indeed, the original Greek meaning of *stereo* is "solid," something stiff, rigid, and hard. And again, we can see how definitions made through design can travel such spectra: something that begins as a prototype becoming a typical example, over time stabilizing to the point of becoming a stereotype. Thus the massive interest in the prototype in design research has good reasons: it is potentially one of the most powerful ways of rebalancing the spectrum of types, counteracting the influence of stereotypes through the making of alternatives. However, it is also clear that not all designing is about the prototypical in this sense: unless the stereotypical is confronted, the making of design prototypes might also end up being about repetition without much significant variation at all. Indeed, we might want to ask: "What do prototypes stereotype?" (cf. Houde and Hill 1997).

Taken together, the program and its typical experiments constitute the programmatic structure's primary stabilizing elements. Once a strong bond has been established between them, it becomes increasingly difficult to find alternative interpretations. It does not matter so much which of them emerges first; they still depend on each other to the extent that they only fully play their parts when both of them have become present. Of course, we can treat our frustration over this relational aspect by devising more or less sequential methods for its treatment—at least as long as we understand that we are addressing nothing but our own frustration. From what we can see in how this spectrum of definitions made through design is structured, there is no *necessary* order for their making, only more or less suitable methods for creating them.

Together the program and the experiments have the potential to create something that neither can do on its own. The resulting assemblage spans an entire section of the spectrum in a way that few—if any—other kinds of definitions in design are able to do. As such, they open up a promising potential for addressing some of our most difficult foundational issues by making new definitions of what designing is.

Life of a Program

Asking "where do programs come from?" or "how does an experiment come about?" is a lot like asking "where do chairs come from?" or "how does one explore different ways of sitting?" And just as giving a general answer, in written form, about how to make chairs is likely to at best result in decent replications of more or less already existing designs, so giving a general answer about how to make a program is not very creative beyond the idea of what programs in general are like. Like making chairs, making programs requires experimentation, training and experience, careful analysis and interpretation of existing examples, and the exploration of alternatives, of different ways of working. It is a bit like trying to answer the question "where do good ideas come from?" Well, they don't really *come* from anywhere; rather, we have to *come up with* them.

By now, we begin to have an idea about the key characteristics of the kinds of definitions made through design that the program and its experiments can result in. While this book is about design theory (what a program or an experiment *is*) and not methods (*how to* work with programs, *how to* make experiments), it could perhaps still be useful to consider how these characteristics come to expression during the life of a program. Thus I would like to end the chapter with an alternative to the account of the opening anecdote.

Conception and Infancy

Whether the research process has its origins in the explicit articulation of a program or emerges as a promising trajectory in open experimentation, the programmatic structure really comes to life only when both components are present—that is, when there is a programmatic lens guiding our understanding of what the experiment exemplifies, and where there is at least one experiment guiding our understanding of what design according to its worldview is like. Such initial experiments may turn out to be *typical* for the program, and even if the first ones are not that typical, we can be sure that typical experiments will emerge early in the process. The reason is that the process itself is so focused on understanding the core of the program, whatever turns out during this phase will be considered "typical" (even if we later realize that other kinds of experiments could also have become typical examples, taking the process in a different direction; indeed, there is nothing inherently *necessary* about design and the directions it takes). We leave this development stage once both program and typical examples have been established and the programmatic research structure is up and running.

Adolescence and Midlife

Having a fairly good idea about what the program is all about, we now turn to explore its central areas. Are there more typical examples? What characterizes them, and how are they similar to, and different from, each other? The program's effectiveness depends on its ability to balance an openness for the unexpected with a strong sense of suggestiveness. As the design process unfolds, we frequently enter situations where we do not quite know what to do, where we encounter conflicting interests stemming from the different perspectives present in a research team or simply from different priorities and agendas. In such situations, we rely on the program to offer some kind of guidance, not so much in terms of what decisions to make, but more importantly in terms of what things to look for, what to pay attention to, and so on. Here the program's worldview is crucial, as it becomes the basis for forming the necessary shared ground, not necessarily in a dogmatic way, but in the sense discussed earlier: that to work, structures operating at this level of abstraction depend on the explicit presence of a basic set of beliefs.

Over time, we develop several different experiments, and we come to create a family of examples.[18] As we create more examples, we also have to confront the issue of repetition, and while a certain amount of repetition serves the purpose of exploring what is *typical* of the program, there is also something problematic about doing the same things over and over again. We have an inherent interest in *difference*, not to mention *change*. And so we start to refute things we know lead to repetition, start to seek edges and boundaries instead, perhaps explicitly addressing questions such as "If this is a typical example of this program, what is then an *atypical* example?" Besides, the research process is not an isolated entity but something that exists in a context where all sorts of factors (external influences and previous experiences included) affect its development. Over time, all these factors cause the entire research process to drift.

We both stay with and stray from our program: things begin to look different as we learn new things, try out new ideas, and explore issues we perhaps have not thought so much about before.

Aging and Death

As the drift caused by both internal and external factors increases over time, it becomes clear that things are no longer the same. We might respond to this insight by becoming conservative, looking toward the center of our program again, seeking ways to stay with it. Or we might realize it is now time to move on, to pick up on those new things we found, and that calls for another programmatic framing to come to full expression. Perhaps we start sketching such a new program in the light of some recent experiment, thinking that what was in the end atypical to our current program is in fact quite typical of what we now see could be done.

Irrespective of our response, these are all indications that the program no longer develops to the same extent. Whether we stay with the program to maintain it or continue into something new, this is a point of closure corresponding to being able to say that we will now answer the question or solve the problem. Because of its character, a closure of this kind of research process might appear less precise than we think an answer to the question would typically be—but then again, that also depends on what kind of question we compare it to (is our comparison to a question like "How high is the Mont Blanc?" or like "How does a clarinet sound?").

Over time, we develop a sense and a sensibility for such closures, and an ability also to recognize them in the work of others, much as we over time develop a basic understanding of what it is, and what it takes, to answer a question or to solve a problem. While we can develop approaches that help us develop such a sensibility, we cannot replace it with a test or procedure (while you can show that you have answered the question of how high a given mountain is, how could you demonstrate that you have a final answer to what a musical instrument sounds like?). And as with questions and problems, so the time it takes to exhaust a program will differ significantly. Some programs will have a short life span; others will last a lifetime.

6 Presenting

Exploring the idea that design research, quite literally, makes definitions through design, we have now looked at three different sets of examples. The first one addressed how such definitions often come in sets and spectra, where conceptual precision is achieved not primarily through making the individual meaning of each notion explicit, but more importantly through how they relate to and differ from each other. The second example showed how complex concepts can be defined *through* design, and in what ways such definitions are at least as powerful and influential as ones of written discourse. And then the last example explored how more complex notions of what designing is (or could be) can be addressed through programs, a kind of structure that engages in matters pertaining to what designing is and how it is carried out, including the basic beliefs and worldviews directing a given way of doing design. Now, to see what difference these ideas might bring to design research, let me revisit the earlier anecdote about examining design research.

Anecdotal Evidence

The opening story was a kind of synthesis from numerous experiences of presenting and representing design research, from serving on review and grading committees, as a discussant and opponent in seminars, as a tutor and supervisor, and so on, presenting, discussing, and analyzing the content and contributions of a piece of research done through design. To recount the story (using a PhD thesis as an example), the presentation of the work begins with an extensive scaffolding, or sampling, of perspectives, concepts, and theories. The resulting assemblage (ideally) shows signs of a basic logic, but we may often question its consistency, as a close reading frequently reveals that quite incompatible positions have been included but not resolved. As a result, we may think that the candidate's reading of, and therefore also *use* of, theory is quite superficial. Then at some point this exposition stops, and a declaration of design intent initiates the transition to the part where the design work, that is, a series of projects or experiments, is described.

This intent or orientation might superficially look like a research question, but it is in reality most of the time more akin to a proposition (which in many cases enforces our previous impression of the candidate's relation to the context of the work, e.g., that she comes with answers, not questions—or, to be more precise, that the basic orientation is inherently propositional in character, not analytical). Such propositions often include some kind of argument regarding what design *could* or *ought to* be.

Following the presentation of the basic trajectory, the experiments or projects are presented, and finally there is a discussion of the results and the experiences gained—but typically there is rarely any substantial engagement with the theoretical background at this stage. Some key concepts may return, others might be used to articulate some findings, but overall we cannot with the best intent call this a complete closure, as so many things are left unanswered and unaddressed. Our initial impression of a weak relation between theory and practice is therefore enforced, and we conclude that there is no real theoretical contribution whatsoever to be found in the work.

Now, this conclusion might well be completely correct. But before we conclude that we are *always* entitled to that conclusion in a situation like this, let me offer an alternative interpretation of what is going on based on the ideas presented in this book. Looking for a pedagogical example, I used a PhD thesis, as it is a piece of work done to demonstrate the ability to individually conduct research, and as such it typically exposes the actual research practice quite unforgivingly.[1] From the perspective of disciplinarity, it is a central form of examination in design research.

Examination

If we start with what the researcher aims to achieve in our example, I would argue that what is basically at stake is a (set of) definition(s) of what designing is; it is about offering an alternative or complementary definition to the set of existing ones. This is a definition made through design, and it is made in the form of a set of particular designs in combination with an overall framing that we can describe as a kind of program. As I have argued, there are reasons for considering aspects of this as belonging to the realm of the theoretical, as these definitions form structures that seem to both perform and function in ways closely resembling how theory works. And so, when we look for the theoretical contributions of the work, it is toward these definitions we need to turn: how they are done, what they entail, and what they imply.

I have argued that such definitions typically must be understood not individually but rather as belonging to various spectra. Precision is achieved not by precise individual positioning but as relative position within a given spectrum, and by populating the spectrum with several *different* definitions. In chapter 3, I used the metaphor of *color* and *a* color to illustrate this idea. One spectrum of definitions of special importance to design stems from the tension between the particular and the general. This spectrum is frequently present in examples such as a PhD thesis, coming to expression through, on one side, a set of definitions of what *a* design is (what we may call design examples or experiments) and, on the other, a definition pushing toward how to understand this kind of design*ing* more generally (what I have called design programs). If we had followed the work more closely as it developed, chances are that we would also have seen other aspects of what I discussed earlier: how initial experiments become projects, how projects become a program as they start addressing matters related to worldviews, how certain examples become "typical," and so on.

The overall result is a kind of composite, or composed, definition spanning a much larger set of issues than any particular kind of concept could do for design. It is an assemblage of definitions that aims toward a meaningful whole, not toward isolated and contained concepts. It is a hands-on way of working with, and explicitly addressing, the tension between the making of the particular and an overall orientation toward the more general *through* design.

It is through *this* assemblage of definitions that the research in question makes its general "theoretical" contribution; and it is when *this* is present that we can say that the process has reached a point of closure and is "finished."

To unpack this idea further, let me again use the shortcomings of my own thesis as an illustration. Halina Dunin-Woyseth and Fredrik Nilsson conducted a project on how to support PhD students developing an understanding of "doctorateness" in architecture, art, and design:

A group of PhD students at the Oslo School of Architecture and Design (AHO) studied an early example of a thesis close to "research by design" (Redström 2001). They commented that it is retrospectively possible to argue that the author's epistemological position may be seen in terms of a by-design or performative paradigm, but that there is a problematical link between practical experimental design and theory in the thesis. Although it is frequently asserted in the thesis that its theories, arguments and design philosophy are based on the results and processes from the practical experimentation, there is little evidence in the actual thesis of how the practical work influenced and shaped the theory:

"The artefacts then act more as illustrations, starting points of discussions by the authors and the presentation of ideas rather than experimental design efforts that in themselves seek to explore, investigate and probe certain topics." (Dunin-Woyseth and Nilsson 2013, 143)

All examples in my thesis started out as experiments, but in my account of them, as I was drifting toward a programmatic approach, I started to treat them in a way that I would now call a kind of definitions. As such, the remark that the artifacts are more similar to illustrations (as when we say, "look at *this* chair") than open experiments (as when reporting on the making a chair, asking "what is sitting?" as we do so) is completely correct; while the design work was like the latter, the articulation of what came out of this process focused on the former. At the time, however, I could not see this difference.

If we extend these two trajectories, we end up in two quite different positions, as we move either toward the idea of design research as a making of definitions or toward describing its open experimentation and problem finding. Typically, we have to account for both dimensions or aspects of our work, but there is also a conceptual trap set by the notion of research *through* design here: if we think that "through design" from an epistemological point of view means that it is the design experimentation as such that this is all about, then we might miss the opportunity to think of the theoretical as an equally viable orientation for how we relate to our results. The theoretical as discussed here is no less about *making* than the hands-on experimentation, but it deals with another aspect of the work, namely, the making of the conceptual.

Indeed, as I have tried to show, many key concepts in design are never precisely articulated in words or text but rather are made *through* design. This is not to be confused with allowing "definitions made through design" to appear from nowhere without properly accounting for how they came about, but just to say that as we account for what they are, we should recognize the important difference between addressing them as unfolding experiments and presenting them as a kind of definition. If we only think of them as a kind of "open" experiment, it is easy to forget that they also act as design definitions with distinct directions and implications.

Figure-Ground

If we instead turn to the issue of the superficial reading of theories from other areas, I would argue that this, if the work is carefully done, can be understood as a building up of the worldview that constitutes the context of the "basic beliefs" of a design program; it is to create and conceptually furnish a place where one can work. Let me try to explain.

As discussed in the previous chapter, the program is not just a declaration of intent (which is what we see on its surface); deeper down, it is the expression of a view on the world, a provisional and incomplete one, but nonetheless a view. This worldview might be close to existing and established ones within the research domain in question, in which case the buildup toward a programmatic framing will contain references familiar to an established way of doing design (research). In a way, we see that the researcher knows her origins and reaffirms key parts of its narrative.

However, this worldview might also contain elements of an alternative to prevalent ways of designing. In such cases, we will see other and typically also more diverse perspectives present, offering different access points to critiquing established and dominant positions. Here it is important to understand that this making up of a worldview has to happen in a different way compared to when someone writes herself into an existing lineage: instead of pointing to similarity and continuity, this account depends on articulating *difference from*. This focus on difference sometimes means that the critical potential of the perspective introduced takes precedence over the consistency of the alternative position pointed to. Indeed, as long as one can critique the target from multiple angles, the precise details of each angle's repercussions considered on their own are of less importance. Or to use another comparison: the relation between program and theoretical background is like *figure-ground*, not like *cause-effect*.

Thus I would argue that a key source of theoretical inconsistency in the background section of our thesis example may stem from how it is oriented toward opening up arguments about difference. This is not an excuse for weak reading, but it explains why certain kinds of inconsistencies do not necessarily stem from not understanding the other perspectives as such, but rather arise from the interpretation (and misinterpretation) of them as ways of exposing aspects of what is being reacted against. This we cannot see if we look toward the inconsistencies as such—here we need to look at the "negative" they form as they come together, knowing that the overall precision of what is being created is to be found elsewhere. But this, as with all things in design, can be done in both the most careful of ways, as well as in the equally reckless.

In most cases, something as extensive as a thesis will have both affirmative and critical components, and thus some sections will build on continuity whereas others will be more disruptive. This often makes it hard to see the different kinds of (in)consistency discussed earlier—but then again, human worldviews are not necessarily only matters of consistency, but also a matter of tension and conflicting concerns. Indeed, if we understand that design seems to thrive on opposing notions and conflicting concepts, then it is likely we will find traces of such inclinations also in its research practices.

If the purpose of the research is to contribute in some form to that other theory, then this approach is not particularly sound—but when that is never the intention, and the real purpose of this engagement is to conceptually furnish a place where one can work, then the situation is somewhat different. Consider Anthony Dunne and Fiona Raby's (2001) notion of "critical design" and its relation to the critical theory of the Frankfurt school. While a term such as "post-optimal object" (Dunne 1999) (of which the previously mentioned Faraday Chair in chap. 3 is a typical example) is meant to be "critical," it is clearly not meant to contribute to that theoretical discourse as such (cf. Dunne and Raby 2013, 34). Rather, it belongs to a history of conversations between design and other domains, including among others the one between Theodor Adorno and Tomás Maldonado mentioned in chapter 2:

The presence of Adorno in Frankfurt represented for me, as it were, a contradictory intellectual stimulus. I have to confess that his impressive speculative fertility, his complicated and somewhat cryptic way of writing, his telling and sometimes provocative aphorisms exerted a fascination on me that was anything but rational: "The useless is eroded, aesthetically inadequate. But the merely useful lays waste the world," he once said to me in an attempt to cool my enthusiasm for the industrial culture of usefulness. … These and other reflections in the spirit of Adorno, and later also Habermas, led me to examine the relationship between industrial culture and the culture industry, and to undertake a critical investigation of the role played by "design" in between these two realities. (Maldonado 1991, 223)

Thus I would argue that it is with respect to such worldviews in design and their development that Dunne and Raby make a theoretical contribution by offering new and alternative notions such as postoptimal objects and design examples such as the Faraday Chair.[2] Reading their work through the lens of critical theory easily obscures this difference, and it may then even appear as if "critical design" was some kind of analytical concept. Indeed, interpreting a definition made through design *as if* it was an analytical definition can lead to all sorts of issues (see for example Bardzell and Bardzell 2013, and then Pierce et al. 2015)—but the fact that we *can* interpret them this way, and therefore also have such conversations, indicates that they indeed do function as definitions.[3]

Based on what we have seen in the examples discussed in the previous chapters—how design makes definitions through design, how we work with fluid concepts and spectra, how design programs allow us to address alternative and provisional design worldviews, and so on—the structure of our initially seemingly problematic example starts to make sense in a different way. We can, of course, deeply disagree with this way of doing design research, thinking that it, especially from a more analytical point of view, is still quite weak when it comes to theory. But there is a crucial difference between thinking that there is no real logic, principle, or structure in place, and thinking that the one employed is not appropriate.

On the Origins Of …

While the previous section dealt with some issues at the level of a particular research effort, let us now consider how such a response fits into a bigger picture. For instance, given my argument that designs can be considered definitions, is not professional practice also then about "knowledge production" in this sense? Indeed, what would be the difference between what we learn in professional practice and the contributions of design research? Such questions have many dimensions, far too many to address in just one way, but let us use the ideas presented here to take a look.

If we start with programs located at the center of a spectrum between product and paradigm and start moving toward the particular, we enter the realm of the project and eventually the product. With respect to new ideas and knowledge, what is really the difference between the designs done in a commercial context and the designs done in the context of research? The initial answer has to be that they are probably not that different at all: a "product" can be a "definition" as influential as anything that comes out of a research process. To illustrate, think of how the Fender Stratocaster (re)defined what an electric guitar is, how the Ford Model T (re)defined what a car is, how the iPhone (re)defined what a telephone is, and so on. Just think of how we use "the" when we point to them: *the* Stratocaster, *the* Ford, *the* iPhone. Our world is full of such definitions of what various kinds of things are.

Importantly, these things come from quite different origins: some of them are artistic works, others commercial products, still others the result of academic research. While knowledge of such origins certainly supports our understanding of them, these "definitions" also tend to have a rather independent existence, many of us not quite knowing where they came from and how. For instance, if I ask you to picture an electric guitar, chances are that the first image that comes to mind is a Fender Stratocaster—but do you actually know its design origins, how it was designed, and for what reasons? It seems that such knowledge is not *necessary* for the Stratocaster to work as a "definition" of what an electric guitar is. Does it really matter if it came out of an academic research process or out of product development if what primarily characterizes it is that it offers a significant design expression of something genuinely *different* from what came before?

The difference between the commercial product and the research experiment is, I think, not possible to account for on the basis that one is a definition made through design whereas the other is not. On the contrary, I think we need to understand that both "kinds" of things can perform in this way. This is also a basic reason why many designers (and indeed also design researchers) do not consider it particularly problematic to relate to both commercial products and academic design research results as "definitions" in their work, as if they were of equal value and quite similar to each other. Although they have different origins, both domains produce crucial definitions that one has to relate to; and at the level of such definitions made through a particular design, the difference in origin is in many cases not that relevant if the definition itself is a strong expression.

This is not to suggest that an object such as the Fender Stratocaster is a kind of design theory. Rather, what I am suggesting is that these definitions, such as of the electric guitar by the Stratocaster, perform as part of the conceptual structures we use to support design. Such definitions should be understood not as theories in themselves but rather as one component alongside others. When we add other components or definitions of more general terms (like the examples of "form" and "user" in chap. 4), programs, and more, then we begin to get something more closely resembling the density of theory. Thus the question is not whether a given design is theoretical or not but rather what role a design understood as a definition made through design may play as part of a larger conceptual structure that we, if the ideas presented here are on to something, need to acknowledge as theoretical in design.

Consider Livework's concept of "service design" as another illustration, and how they explain its origins in this interview by Bill Moggridge:

We needed to have a language to speak about services in a native way; we realized that we wanted to have a connection to the academic community, so that we could test our thinking rigorously; and we needed some big clients that would buy service design projects.

We've been building service design from a series of different academic disciplines. We've looked at academic theory about how value-nets operate; we've been drawing on anthropological work from human-computer interaction, and we've taken everything we could from interaction design, and put all this together in what we call "service design." (Moggridge 2007, 417)

Although the statement clearly describes a matter of professional design, we can see many of the characteristics of research through design that I have been discussing: how a definition of a complex notion, in this case service design, is made at several different levels in parallel. At the level of the particular, we see references to projects with clients (some of which would turn out to be *typical* examples), we see the building up of a kind of worldview in relation to which the design intent can be articulated (and also here we see connections to a diverse set of areas not normally connected to each other as academic disciplines), and we see a set of (new) basic terms that help to articulate what design*ing* is ("a language to speak about services in a native way"). Indeed, some of these terms have become central to how we articulate and understand service design, such as "touch-points," "evidencing," and "blueprinting." All of these ideas have similarities with notions already in use in design, but they have become important because they also introduced something different.

Another example could be the Apple Macintosh as defined through the "Human Interface Guidelines" (Apple Computer 1992). This document not only provides an account of how a given product has been designed; it is also a design program for what using a computer can be like, along with many concepts that describe what designing such things should be like: "You can find out how to incorporate good human interface into your design and decision-making processes and how to involve users throughout the design process. You can also read about how to work with and go beyond the guidelines while maintaining their spirit and intent" (1).

Given examples such as this (and there are many), I think we have little to gain from an argument of difference based on the context in which the work happens, be it commercial or academic. Instead we need to look toward the structure of the work, and to what extent it is oriented toward providing new and alternative definitions of what *a* design and what design*ing* are. This approach may appear to completely disregard aspects such as the rigor that is required of academic research—and with respect to this particular aspect, it does: if the new definitions express significant and important difference, it seems we are likely to use them to articulate matters of design quite independently (well, of course, some sources are far more influential than others, but still) of where they originally came from.[4] That said, it is unlikely that anyone makes such expressive new definitions without being rigorous in terms of design and designing: one does not consistently achieve precision, depth, and difference by chance. Again, it seems we are looking at something more akin to a continuous spectrum than discrete dichotomies.

Looking the Other Way

While commercial design may sometimes take on the task of achieving such conceptual precision and depth, these qualities are more frequently an objective in research. Indeed, an important clue to how academic research differs from most commercial work in this regard can be found in the frequent remarks about research prototypes "not being finished." A remark like this may sound like an apologetic defense of a final finish far from what we what expect from prototypes made for commercial contexts, but the more profound reason for the design researcher to typically spend much less time on a design's details is that research prototypes are often "just" examples or illustrations of something, not ends in themselves. Certainly, they have importance as designs, as well, but if there is something to the ideas presented here, they need to be understood as parts of a larger effort, a programmatic construction. Thus what level of resolution they need to have depends not so much on the intended function or use of the object as on what level of detail is needed for it to perform its role, to express the *difference it makes*, within the overall context of the design program. Unlike a product that needs to function on its own out there, the research prototype is typically not meant to live an independent life outside its programmatic context.

And so when one hear remarks along the lines of "whereas professional design aims to resolve matters of, say, functionality, utility, or aesthetics, design research prototypes aim for new 'knowledge,'" this is actually a rather confused argument. New knowledge might be the intended outcome of research—but as discussed earlier, the difference between the commercial product and the research prototype cannot be understood on the principle of one making a contribution to what we *know* about design whereas the other does not.

To understand the difference that research through design aims to make, we must instead turn to the other direction in our spectrum: toward *practice* and *paradigm*. In the previous chapter, I discussed how a program's basic beliefs have to be more exposed and less internalized compared to how they may appear in practice, pointing to their potential use as a kind of prototype of alternative worldviews; but there are still many questions about how this may or may not contribute to our more general understanding of what designing is. Indeed, a programmatic approach can appear to rather violently cut big issues into pieces, reducing open and general questions to particularities (indeed, the fundamental tension between the particular and the universal is always present).

First, we need to acknowledge that programmatic research through design will have to be just one of many ways in which we try to understand and articulate what design*ing*, in general, is. The way that such research contributes to design theory is extremely particular, and there is both space and need for other ways of asking similar, as well as completely different, questions (e.g., Tonkinwise 2014). That said, I would argue that the kind of research discussed here offers something quite important. Let us first return to the picture of the many programs of the previous chapter.

With respect to the issue of foundations, we can see that while the picture emerging through the many programs is fragmentary, these programs nevertheless represent a way of populating more foundational levels.

In design, we do not have Circle, we have circles; we do not have Chair, we have chairs. Similarly, programmatic design research produces only fragments of foundations, pieces that rely on other such pieces to form something akin to a field rather than a singular vantage point. As such, they seek to address the tension between a need for foundations, on the one hand, and the problem of static generalizations, on the other. The "knowledge" of what designing, in general, is all about that we get here is fragmented, but as I have argued throughout, an ambition to achieve a cohesive and consistent overall theoretical model is, in the realm of design, *also* problematic.

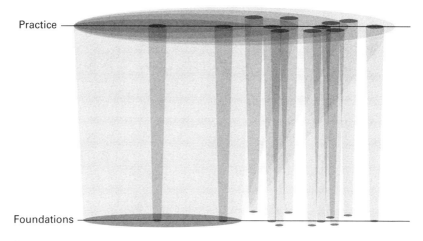

Figure 6.1
Many design research programs …

Practice

Foundations

Figure 6.2
... potentially creating new transitional foundations.

Presenting Alternatives

With respect to what we may learn from research through design, there is one particular potential I would like to address. Underlying most conceptions of "change" or "problem solving" is the idea that design somehow is about bringing about a (better) future. Ranging from optimistic narratives of infinite progress expressed as slogans of global consumerism, opportunities, and innovation, to accounts of the utter unsustainability of Western ways of living at the ruin of all, we generally think of design as offering ways of looking forward. Bolstered by an inherently positive attitude toward change, we often tell stories not only of looking forward but of looking forward *to*.

At the same time, as Dunne and Raby put it, "Design's inbuilt optimism can greatly complicate things, first, as a form of denial that the problems we face are more serious than they appear, and second, by channeling energy and resources into fiddling with the world out there rather than the ideas and attitudes inside our heads that shape the world out there" (Dunne and Raby 2013, 2). This puts notions of speculative and conceptual design, design about ideas, at the forefront as ways to probe and provoke the domains of values and worldviews: "We need more pluralism in design, not of style but of ideology and values" (9). Given design's strong orientation toward making understood as material production, the realm of the speculative and the conceptual might appear as less "real," but we have only to look at the world to see just how real are the effects of our values and worldviews.

Since "futures" once again seem to be the new black in design, I would therefore like to look at how we relate to notions of "future" in design. In particular, I argue that design programs may be able to address this idea in a way quite different from what needs to be done when you start with what is already established as *practice*.

In the late 1970s, Norman Henchey (1978) distinguished between probable, preferable, plausible, and possible futures to account for different approaches to future studies. Later expressed as a cone-shaped diagram by Trevor Hancock and Clem Bezold (1994), and then others (e.g., Voros 2003), the image of futures has become a reference point in design, as well (e.g., Dunne and Raby 2013).

The diagram illustrates different kinds of paths forward, where moving more or less straight ahead is the most *probable*. Within what is at all *possible*, however, we also find what is still *plausible*—and somewhere in this, we need to place the trajectory that we believe is *preferable*. We may then ask questions about what it is necessary to do in the present to make that preferable future come into being. We can compare this image with ideas about design presented around the same time, such as Herbert Simon's "Everyone designs who devises courses of action aimed at changing existing situations into preferred ones" (1996, 111), or John Chris Jones's "The effect of designing is *to initiate change in man-made things*" (1992, 4). In the diagram, as well as in such ideas about designing, the basic concept is one of moving forward, our actions being ways to affect the direction, design as change of course. As with any abstract diagram or general idea, however, the apparent simplicity should not be confused with the underlying complexity; this is just a way of mapping general characteristics.

The first feature I would like to turn to is that the diagram starts in a point: "now" is one, a singular position. When we look toward established ways of doing things, toward practices, it may seem as if now is indeed a point, a *state*. But as we look toward the future, it is clear that this now is not one. For instance, as can be seen in the debates on the matter, the now of a market strategist investigating the global consumer market looking at probable, plausible, and preferable futures of the next product line is not

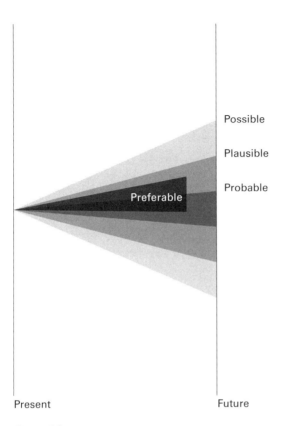

Possible

Plausible

Probable

Preferable

Present   Future

Figure 6.3
Futures.

necessarily the now of the climate researcher looking at probable futures in the light of overconsumption of resources; the now of the design researcher thinking about the futures of electronic devices and digital materials is not necessarily the now of the person working with retrieving rare metals at a hazardous e-waste dump. And so, as we reflect on the state of the world, on the vast differences between these positions, their perspectives, the presence and absence of privileges, and so on—the things we now know we need to change—how could now ever be *a point*?

As we look once more at the now expressed as a point and design's inherent enthusiasm for what could be, the diagram shifts from being an image of how the future continuously opens up, to become an illustration of our tunnel vision.

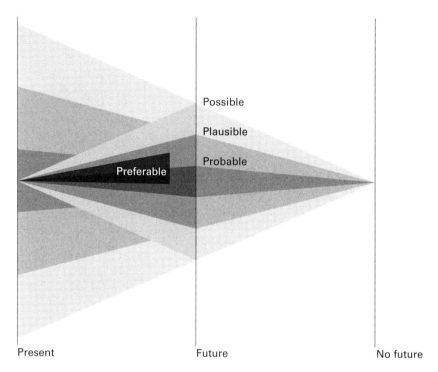

Present   Future   No future

Figure 6.4
No futures.

Because we do not take into account the wider field of perspectives, we also fail to see what Tony Fry (2009) has called "defuturing" by design, how design's interventions into the world destroy futures as much as create them. Taking a broader look at all our nows, trying to look beyond our own immediate situation, we might well face a state of "no future" rather than an ever-expanding space of possibilities ahead of us. Standing at this *one* point, we have little chance of seeing whether we face an open cone of possible futures, or if it is really a tunnel vision ending with a point, a definitive punctuation mark.

Importantly, this is not an argument about the need for inclusion. Rather, it is about the risk of occlusion as we try to look toward our common future. What is needed is not that we make our own point bigger by somehow making it include more; it will still be just a point and not a field.[4] Rather, the conclusion to draw from this picture is that we have a basic responsibility for not occluding others.

Futuring and Presenting

Research through design can respond to this issue in many different ways depending on what parts of the spectrum between the particular and the general one targets. While challenges such as social and environmental sustainability call for new perspectives across the entire spectrum, we still need to start somewhere.

One strategy is to start with existing practices and find ways of redirecting them. Tony Fry (2009) describes this as "futuring" design, that is, setting new trajectories for how design (and thus all the impacts of design's interventions) develops and effectively creates a more sustainable future. As shown by Fry and others, the possibilities of redirecting design practice, as well as using design to redirect other kinds of practices, are significant (e.g., Fry 2009; Shove et al. 2007; Mazé et al. 2011; Pierce et al. 2013). With respect to the ideas presented in this book, however, I would like to use these issues as a backdrop for discussing an alternative approach in the light of the differences between practice and program: if practices require redirective action in the form of *futuring*, working with programs could instead be about *present-ing* alternatives.

When I presented the idea of programs in chapter 5, I argued that they offer interesting possibilities when it comes to working with the basic beliefs, or worldviews, of design*ing*. These possibilities emerge as we move from the particular toward the general across the spectrum and into the area of programs where issues related to worldviews become more central, but also because matters related to our "basic beliefs" are much more exposed and fragile in programs compared to how they appear as internalized and hidden in practice. With respect to redirecting designing, this has two important implications: first, rather than being a matter of unpacking something already in place, the program calls for an explicit articulation of intent that cannot be taken for granted; and second, these worldviews, therefore, do not have be something already existing. In other words, there is a kind of "what if" character to programs that sets them apart from practices.

Looking back at our two-layered cones, we could think about programs as a way to create alternative nows, as a matter of populating a wider base with examples of how things could be different—not in the future but *now*. When working with redirecting what already exists, the key concern is the altering of trajectories, and thus change needs to be understood in terms of futuring. But if we think of design research as a matter of *making difference* rather than as *change*, then design programs could allow us to explore different starting points for defining what designing is.

There is little reason to understand design research as strictly committed to futures, although the narratives of technological progress coupled with design's optimistic outlook certainly exercise a strong influence in that direction. Design research addressing matters such as attitudes, values, and behaviors, does not necessarily depend on future technologies or opportunities to be possible. On the contrary, it depends on questioning what is now, asking what if things were already different (cf. Hickey, Köpplin, and Tremonte 2012).

Within a program, we are free to say that things are indeed different: we are free to state that *all* design is to be done on the basis of the geometry of the circle, the square, and the triangle, though we know that the world does not look like that; we are free to say that designing is all about doing away with things, though we know that existing design practice typically works with the opposite; and so on. While certainly neither politically nor poetically independent from their contexts, programs have a different relation to existing conditions than practices have, and in particular they are not tied to working on the basis of futures in the same way. We do not have to think about designing as a matter of changing course, about altering an already-established trajectory; we can also think of it as a matter of *presenting* alternatives, of making a more diverse set of possible nows more *present*.

One might object that while this might be true, letting go of the idea of initiating actual change also implies that such design research becomes an academic exercise with little real impact. But if the analysis of how design develops over time—from products and projects via programs to practices—tells us something about what is actually going on, then the transition from program to practice is one of the things we need to keep an eye on with respect to redirecting design. When I first introduced the notion of programs as part of this spectrum of definitions of what a design and of what designing is, I used the example of the educational program. Educational programs are perhaps the most important tool we have for preparing for practice, for training to enter professional practice. Design research programs can work in a similar way—with the important difference that we can train ourselves, prepare for practice, fail miserably over and over, get up again and try something else, working with a wide variety of programs, most of which will never turn into actual practices. And when we think we have something worthwhile, only then do we let it become part of actual practice.

We need ways of learning from working with definitions of designing where we explore the implications of various worldviews, and where there is a real possibility that the program brings about a kind of design that should not be taken further. If we take the presence of many nows seriously, there are few reasons for thinking that a design project or program is "successful" in a more general sense just because it meets success criteria such as being picked up in professional practice. If there was ever a need for devices such as the "design laboratory," then surely this must be part of it: to explore different ways of designing and really push their characteristics to learn something without causing collateral damage. Because if design is about a "service relationship" (Nelson and Stolterman 2012, 41), then for design to fail is also for design *to fail someone*. In a sense, the design inquiry starts not from a premise but with a promise. Importantly, the notion of a promise is not only about the risk of failing, but also about hope.

Consistency or Consensus

Design programs can be used to explore what designing according to a certain worldview is like, to learn from it, to understand its implications—and to do this, we do not have to make it "real." It might be that the most important contributions of research through design to the issue of redirecting practice are made not in terms such as "change" or "futures" but in the realm of a wider set of differences or alternative nows that help counteract tendencies of tunnel vision and destabilize the idea that now can be conceived as a single point. But while working with a multitude of programs can offer an alternative to approaches aiming toward one dominant point or position, it is also necessary for such research to be grounded and conducted in different contexts, conditions, and cultures to actually achieve this goal.

When it comes to our existing design methodology, we might therefore ask: what are, *really*, the implications of having a basic frame of reference that is fundamentally oriented toward notions of convergence? As in John Chris Jones's (1992) three-stage process of divergence–transformation–convergence, or the seemingly ubiquitous "double-diamond" model of design (Design Council 2007)? An orientation toward convergence certainly serves a purpose when our objective is to provide *a* solution to *a* problem, or when we aim to create *one* prototype that will form the basis of mass production. But what does such an orientation bring to our overall understanding of what design is and does (cf. Karlsson and Redström 2016)? To what extent are diversity and pluralism at all possible within a methodological framework so fundamentally oriented toward *convergence*?

If we add to this an ambition from design research to move toward unified theory (because we are led to believe that this is what science aims for), eventually converging on a certain set of concepts, definitions, models, and so on—where do all of these position us with respect to the inherent normative character of design? Even when arguing for a *science* of the artificial, Herbert Simon (1996) could not avoid speaking about how things *ought* to be.

Much of this book has been about showing how certain conceptual structures used in design become defined, how they are given a direction. To orient such forms of making toward some idea about unified theory—to make them converge by harmonizing definitions and directions—would also be to make them point to the same ideas about how things ought to be. There is a real risk of confusing conceptual consistency with some kind of ideological or political consensus here. If we instead would use the ways we already seem to orient toward notions of difference to embrace pluralism and diversity, then it might be possible to open up a kind of transparency and accountability that allows us to more openly debate not what things ought to be like but what we hope them to become.

Design differs from science, but Karen Barad's remark on realism is still equally valid:

"Objectivity" is not preexistence (in the ontological sense) or the preexistent made manifest to the cognitive mind (in the epistemological sense). Objectivity is a matter of accountability for what materializes, for what comes to be. It matters which cuts are enacted: different cuts enact different materialized becomings. (Barad 2007, 361)

7 Transitional Theory

This book opened with the suggestion that as design research engages in the making of many different kinds of things, design theory might well be one of those things it could be making. Whereas a theory *of* design would take design and designing as its subject, the notion of *design theory* seems to call for an inquiry into theory as something developed in and through design. Following this idea, I have been asking questions about what such forms of making theory could be like and what the results might look like. This led to an exploration of conceptual elements and structures in research through design that, although they do not *look* like the kinds of theory we are familiar with from other domains, still seem to work and function in design in ways closely related to what theory normally does for its domain.

However, this inquiry presented a certain methodological problem. Since a theory is never just a theory but always *a* theory *of* something, and the concern was not a theory *of* design but the potential of design theory made through practice, I somehow had to find another way of addressing the issue of directedness. The obvious solution would be to pick a topic, such as aesthetics, and sketch out such a theory of this topic, for example, to *make* a design theory of aesthetics and work with it as an example. This approach would, however, risk dramatically shifting the center of gravity away from the more general characteristics of the making of such conceptual components and structures as such and instead become about the resulting theory itself. Thus, to address this aspect of directedness, that theories are theories *of*, I decided to look for ways in which we create and manage such orientations and directions. One of the most central ways we do so, in any kind of theory, is through basic definitions. And so, instead of starting with providing the basic definitions necessary for developing a theory of something, I focused on how definitions come about, and in particular on asking questions regarding if, and if so *how*, we make basic definitions of key concepts through design. Indeed, as Nietzsche put it already in 1885:

What dawns on philosophers last of all: they must no longer accept concepts as a gift, nor merely purify and polish them, but first make and create them, present them and make them convincing. Hitherto one has generally trusted one's concepts as if they were a wonderful dowry from some sort of wonderland: but they are, after all, the inheritance from our most remote, most foolish as well as most intelligent ancestors. (Nietzsche 1968, §409)

Thus a key idea here is that to *do* design theory is not to introduce or articulate the use of long-since-established terms in the context of design and designing but rather to, once again, make and create them. In this book, I have therefore tried to outline an answer to how design theory could be *made* in design research. Focusing on three different and seemingly crucial ways in which such theoretical components and structures are made through design, I then tried to map out some key characteristics of what this making is like.

The first set of examples (chap. 3) illustrated how we use combinations of terms to address continuous spectra by means of differences between them rather than trying to isolate each term on its own on the basis of its essence. Besides being able to cope with complexity in ways that discrete terms are not able to on their own, this way of working with definitions also seemed to allow the terms to stay open for change, and thus be able to follow an unfolding design process. Since this means leaving aside more familiar criteria for conceptual precision based on what is stable over time, I used examples, such as how we deal with color, to illustrate that orientations toward discrete and static definitions probably comes down to intellectual habits rather than actual requirements of design theory.

The second set of examples (chap. 4) showed how more complex notions can be made through design. Working with notions that we use to articulate what design is about (form), and for whom it is done (users), I aimed to show how more abstract concepts can be defined through design in ways at least as powerful and influential as by any written counterpart in research discourse. Inquiring into the effects of making foundational definitions rigid and stable in design, I argued that confusing conceptual precision for stability introduces a significant risk that such concepts may not be able to support development and cope with change. While we are certainly able to create stable definitions through design, we should in principle also be able to create more dynamic alternatives. To exemplify what such alternatives could be like, I introduced ways of defining form and user that instead aimed for the transitional and unstable. As such, this set of examples included ways of making both stable and unstable definitions of more complex terms to show that such aspects of design theory are within reach of what can be made through design.

The third way of making theoretical structures was design research programs (chap. 5). As discussed here, a program is a way of dealing with complexity in design by means of creating a kind of composite definition of what designing is. Programs are complex sociomaterial assemblages, but from this design theoretical point of view, they can be said to center on the unfolding relations between program and experiment. In particular, programs allow us to work with matters pertaining to worldviews, the basic sets of beliefs that designing depends on, but which are rarely made explicit in practice. Programs also serve to connect the basic definitions we make through design to methodology, and as such they can be considered a kind of conceptual structure that allows us to address matters of discipline, or disciplining, in design, including questions such as what makes something typical, or why something is excluded and considered to be the matter of something else.

Taken together, these three different ways of making theoretical components and structures provide a considerable repertoire of possibilities for us to address matters of design theory, and as such they provide a basis for the continuous creation of a kind of "transitional theory." If "design theory" refers to what we use to conceptualize, understand, and articulate design and designing, then "transitional" refers to the way in which these ideas do so. Avoiding the static criteria so characteristic of how we normally think about conceptual precision, what has been presented here is instead full of inherently fluid notions and becoming structures. And while this means we have sacrificed certain forms stability, we seem to have gained something that comes prepared to cope with continuous change.

Thus, this book is not about theorizing design transitions or transitioning (cf. Kossoff, Irwin, and Willis 2016) but about the characteristics of the theories as such. These ideas, concepts, principles—*theories*—are transitional in a sense similar to the notion of transitional forms in evolutionary biology: traces of how a form has evolved into another, as in transitional forms showing how life evolved from living in water to living on land. They are transitional in a sense similar to the notion of transitional objects in psychoanalysis: objects such as the child's blanket providing comfort and support during the process of developing an understanding of the external world, as when grappling with the "not-me," of experiencing the parent as external to the self (cf. Winnicott 1953; Attfield 2000). They are transitional in a sense similar to Wittgenstein's ladder:[1] propositions that are used to obtain a different view but in retrospect are no longer *necessary*. And they are transitional in a sense related to Gilles Deleuze's "intellectually mobile concepts," to how "all the new sports—surfing, windsurfing, hang-gliding—take the form of entering into an existing wave. There's no longer an origin as starting point, but a sort of putting-into-orbit. The key thing is how to get taken up into the motion of a big wave" (Deleuze 1995, 121).

Projections

While most theory deals with what exists, theory does not in principle abide to the temporal condition of following from known fact—at least not in any trivial notion of "following." As discussed previously, any account of how experimentation *follows* from theory or vice versa is bound to fail; the relations between them are complicated and above all diverse. Indeed, although most of what we think about when talking about theory deals with matters we can relate to as being in one way or another already given or existing, there is also a trace of theater here (also etymologically), of what is not quite real—at least not yet. Theory is used not only to account for existing things but also importantly to imagine things not yet seen. We use theory to predict events and phenomena, such predictions even becoming the basic rationale for enormous long-term investments in experimental setups to find out whether this is actually the case or not (as with the Large Hadron Collider at CERN, e.g.).

While the temporal independence and interdependence of theory, exploration, and experiment open up a vast array of research perspectives, our transitional design theories are different from most in that they are also temporal in themselves. They are not timeless, and their life cycle is not characterized by development from hypothesis, through proper functioning and increasing refinement, to death and dissolution because something more precise comes along to replace it. They differ from the more ordinary working hypothesis in that their typical trajectory is not one of becoming ever more precise and stable, eventually becoming theory proper.

The conceptual structures discussed here are deeply temporal in that they become meaningful and precise only in relation to designing. Of course, we can abstract from this, taking a step outside, looking at design as something given, and talk about our terms and concepts *as if* they were static and stable; but as I have tried to show, this is inherently problematic if it is unfolding design development we aim to support. Like any picture, it is a fixed moment in time—and as such it quickly becomes part of the articulation of history rather than the making of futures. And while history is also essential to design, being "historical" in the sense of conceptual fossilization will not help us understand what we now can and need to do.

Definitions

With respect to basic definitions in design theory, two remarks I made in the introduction set the trajectory for what has followed. First, that we lack unified definitions—we do not even have a shared basic definition of what "design" actually is—is not a problem that design theory should seek to resolve. Rather, I have argued that this absence is indicative of design's condition. And second, we need to look into the making of definitions in design, since definitions are one of the primary ways in which theory becomes *a* theory *of* something. As such, definitions are basic building blocks of theory, and thus their making is a key to understanding how more complex and extensive structures can be created. In the inquiry that followed, however, something else emerged that cast the ways definitions are made in design in a partly new light: when our interests turn toward change and to making a difference, our concepts seem to follow suit and drift away from the issues of essence that so often take center stage in how we think about what it means to be explicit.

In contrast to how we normally start *from* definitions, the actual acts of defining are central in more or less all the examples I have discussed. I obviously labor under a rather suspicious conception of theory in the first place (then again, we will always have "and so how would you *define* design theory—and what do you *assume* about design and designing when offering that definition?"), but to make the most of the argument I have presented here, we should consider it as the design inquiry it is: *What if* research through design would develop theories; what would they then be like? As such, it asks us to, at least for a moment, accept its premise—or, in the light of design described as a service relationship (Nelson and Stolterman 2012), perhaps better, its promise—to see what spectacle we are wandering to witness.

If by "theory" we refer to the various concepts and ideas, as well as the structure, logic, or ordering of such concepts and ideas, that we use to understand, describe, predict, control, and so on, something, then there are reasons for thinking about certain components of research through design as highly theoretical. Not because these components have the same form as the theories we are used to in other disciplines, but because they seem to perform in similar ways, and for similar reasons. Perhaps what I refer to as different kinds of "definitions made through design" is just another way of articulating certain ways that the inherent propositional character of the artificial comes to expression, but even so, I would argue that there are both structural similarities and important interactions between the examples discussed here and what more analytically inclined disciplines refer to as their theories. Indeed, I believe that this is something we somehow need to acknowledge and articulate if we are to account for how research through design works, and if we are serious about challenging the dichotomy between theory and practice—and the division of labor it sustains—that we at some point inherited from a very different time and place.

Even if I had used the term "proposition" instead of "definition" to articulate much of what has been addressed here, it would not have captured the way these things perform in quite the same way. Consider completely letting go of the idea that what we offer are different definitions of what design is, and instead just refer to them as different propositions. Would that help? It would certainly cast the idea of "unified theory" in a different light, as an ambition to achieve "unified propositions" sounds far less exciting. At the same time, however, it certainly feels as if something more is at stake here. Consider a more concrete definition made through design: having created this object for you to sit on, I can, of course, *present* it by saying, "I'd like to *propose* that this is a chair," but this is not quite the same as to say, "This *is* a chair." This is complicated, however, and it is certainly possible to move in the direction of design as rhetoric instead, designing considered as a matter of persuasion, a design an argument in material form (cf. Buchanan 1985; Seago and Dunne 1999; Redström 2006a). But while such perspectives are useful for understanding certain aspects of what design is and does, it is more difficult to use them for understanding the knowledge, ideas, and concepts developed through design more generally, and what happens in activities like research through design in particular.

Of course, there are also elements of persuasion in design research, but when we relate to the designs of others, to their alternative design programs and worldviews, to other ways of understanding and performing general notions such as "form," these designs are more than a kind of argument to us. Perhaps we can see the argument in them, their persuasive elements, but we also see much more. Picking up the clarinet, our fingers finding their way even as we do not quite know where to put them, then lightly blowing into the mouthpiece, trying to make a sound, and listening to the sounds we are making: is not our most immediate experience "so *this* is what the clarinet is like?

The encounter with the musical instrument is not only a matter of the persuasive dimensions of a proposition, of acting in relation to a script materialized through design, but also one of coming to know what *this thing is*, the "propositionality" of the instrument primarily being that it has been *made* and therefore could also have been made *differently*. This is not to say that the musical instrument cannot be considered an argument, its design a matter of scripts, but to say that, at least, it is *also* a definition of what a clarinet is, and consequently, when we are asked about how the clarinet sounds, we can answer that we now *know*.[2]

The clarinet might be an unfair example, both because musical instruments are not the most typical things designers make, and because clarinets have a highly defined form (though the variations within this form, to the trained musician, are substantial; not every violin is a Stradivarius). But is this situation really that different from someone's experience of first starting to use a smartphone instead of the old camera as her primary tool for taking pictures? Or, to look at particular material aspects of the design of cameras, how the very act of taking a photograph changed when the viewfinder was replaced with a display on the back, or how the ways we produce, process, and share images changed with the replacement of film by digital imaging. Or the first time someone rides a mountain bike down a trail where his ordinary street bike would inevitably make the emergency room his next stop (not saying he didn't end up there anyway).

These experiences of when a familiar category is (partially) redefined by a new design are individual and of course dependent on one's previous encounters with that category. While it is difficult to see a familiar thing we take for granted, like a camera, a bike, or a mobile phone, as a kind of ongoing and highly active "definition" of what these things are to us, is there not a glimpse of this idea in the experience of something familiar being redefined through the introduction of a significant difference? "So *this* is a camera," "I have never experienced biking like *that* before," "I would never have thought that phones would become *this*," and so on.[3]

Looking at how we approach such terms, how they receive more specific meaning in the context of designing and using, I have argued that calling them out as definitions might be the best fit when comparing what they do, and how they do it, to how other disciplines understand and use their theories. That we *also* see that they are inherently propositional, is—I would argue—not primarily a matter of the concepts or their structures as such, but rather yet another reflection of the fundamental condition of designing: that the artificial is *never necessary*.

When our objective is to uncover and articulate the general, the exception becomes a problem, a disturbance or nuisance. In statistical analysis, for instance, extreme outliers are more likely to be considered extraneous experimental errors than actual data. Indeed, when studying what is, what is created during the process of observation is often considered a problem—and thus the notion of "artifact" is used, along with other notions such as noise, to denote errors stemming from the experimental setup. When we turn to the artificial, to the *artifact* not as error but as intention, the issue of exception is also reversed. Consider expressions such as "an *exceptional* design," "an *outstanding* design." With respect to making definitions through design, is this not an expression that captures precisely how a design not only follows the rule, thus being identifiable as belonging to a given category, but also at the same time transcends it, becoming an *exception, standing outside* what was previously given? It is the act of moving beyond through the making of a significant *difference* that forms the basis for how designs are able to define and redefine how we understand what a given kind or category is.

I have tried to show that we might be making and using our conceptual structures in ways very similar to how we make and use other kinds of "designs" in design research. That we do not settle for just one definition of design is not because we do not understand the essence of design, but because it is much more powerful to work with difference as a basis when coping with complexity and change. And to work on the basis of (making a) difference, we need alternatives, and we need diversity. This is still a conversation between us about what design *is*, but it is one centered on its potentials for change, not its eventual convergence.

Structures

The book opened with a remark that design seems to thrive on dichotomies, that the space opened up inside the tension between conflicting conceptions somehow seems to speak to how the design situation often requires negotiation of opposing tendencies, be it between the particular and the universal, between taking a lead and being of service, between art and science ... Similar to such productive tensions, the one between static and transitional requires a more nuanced position than merely choosing between firm stability and constant change.

As much as we like to do new things in life, we also appreciate that certain things can be taken for granted. Indeed, living without memory, where every daily activity appears as if it is being done for the first time, is a most frightening condition. From its industrial origins in the shop and assembly line, design, like so many other areas of human conduct, inherited a strong bias toward understanding what is rational as what can be repeated, each time delivering a reliable result. Designing surely needs its routines, its *methods*—but as I have discussed, there are important differences between foundations for explaining regularities and what is needed for making a difference. Ironically, there are strong bonds between our historical amnesia and contemporary conceptual fossilization.

Structurally, the book, as well as each chapter, follows the perhaps most typical form of inductive analysis: that of first presenting a situation or issue that needs to be resolved, and then moving on to develop the ideas and concepts, the *theories*, needed to address it—although the rather sarcastic term "anecdotal evidence" signals that we are probably not about to find any induction proper. However, the book *also* follows forms typical of research through design, as in how its basic approach is based on initial experiments probing certain issues and proceeding to make a series of "prototypes" to get to an understanding of what this is all about. I have tried to show how theory development in research through design could be structurally similar to working with other kinds of design expressions and outcomes.

At times, it seems as if when we need our design premise/promise to come forth like a research question to be answered or a problem to be solved, we turn it into one; if we need our design inquiry to look like analysis, we at least superficially make it follow such forms. This is not to say that there cannot be genuine analysis in design, or there are no proper research questions to answer, significant problems to solve, and so on—only that it is *also* far too easy to relate to various forms of inquiry in a superficial way, and it therefore is dangerous to think that how research is presented is indicative of how it actually works.

Importantly, therefore, this book can be read as a concrete instance of the ideas it presents: this book is in itself an example of programmatic design research, transitional theory being the program, with ideas such as the alternative definitions of terms like form or use being *typical* examples. The conclusion is inevitable:

This is an example.

Notes

Chapter 1

1. The idea of this book as a picture might appear ironic given that it is only sparsely illustrated. The primary reason behind the limited visual material is, however, neither the complexities of copyright nor the costs of printing, but more importantly the ways in which images tend to work in design discourse—a topic addressed at some length in chapter 4 and with the notion of image as definition. Thus, instead of extensive visual material, this book comes with a heartfelt recommendation to visit museums and archives, to see different images, and most importantly to really attend to the things when actually encountered (whether in someone's home, a public place, a museum, or somewhere else).

Chapter 2

1. For an illustration of this conceptual drift, see the interview with Frayling by representatives from the "Research through Design" conference series, http://researchthroughdesign.org/provocations (accessed October 21, 2016).

2. In the institutional contexts of design research, artistic research is primarily articulated in terms of knowledge production. For instance, in the Research Assessment Exercise (RAE) of the United Kingdom, "'Research' for the purpose of the RAE is to be understood as original investigation undertaken in order to gain knowledge and understanding" (RAE2008 2006, 80); or by the Swedish Research Council, "Research, regardless of art form, is practice-based and includes intellectual reflection aimed at developing new knowledge," http://vr.se/inenglish/shortcuts/artistic research.4.5adac704126af4b4be2800011077.html (accessed October 21, 2016).

3. About the origins and objectives of HFI, as stated in the first report: "The Home Research Institute (HFI), founded by the Swedish housewives' and home economics teachers' joint organizations in 1944, studies consumption and life within the home, the work of housewives, and the division of labor between households and industry, as well as methods and utensils for domestic work. The HFI also aims to

provide guidelines for a satisfactory production of consumer goods, such as house-hold objects and utensils, food and clothes, and instructions for facilitating and rationalizing domestic work, and material for education and information for homes, schools and institutional housekeeping" (my translation) (Hemmens Forskningsin-stitut 1946).

4. For some of its early beginnings, see Smets and Overbeeke 1994.

5. Or, more precisely: it is actually quite easy to make a definition of what design or designing is, but difficult to reach consensus about it. As I argue later, that this is so is significant; the issue with properly *defining* design is not that definitions differ but that we somehow think we need to reach consensus in the matter, that one defini-tion should rule over the others.

Chapter 3

1. "DeSForM: Design and Semantics of Form and Movement," Northumbria School of Design, https://www.northumbria.ac.uk/about-us/academic-departments/ northumbria-school-of-design/research/desform (accessed October 21, 2016).

2. Indeed, as I try to show in later chapters, there are reasons (some even pertain-ing to "routine") to address design as praxis rather than as poiesis, although the latter certainly holds potential for what we want design to be like. To Aristotle, praxis seems primarily tied to the doings and routines of work and life, whereas poiesis is a matter of making in the light of understanding, reflecting, searching—of bringing-forth and revealing, as Martin Heidegger would have it: "It is of utmost importance that we think bringing-forth in its full scope and at the same time in the sense in which the Greeks thought it. Not only handicraft manufacture, not only artistic and poetical bringing into appearance and concrete imagery, is a bringing-forth, *poiesis*. ... Through bringing-forth the growing things of nature as well as whatever is completed through the crafts and the arts come at any given time to their appearance. ... Bringing-forth brings out of concealment into un-con-cealment" (Heidegger 2008, 317; see also Dilnot 2015, 143–144). For now, however, I will remain with the notion of practice, as this is the term we typically use when talking about design.

3. One could perhaps make similar observations about how the approach to aes-thetics developed at HfG Ulm, its inherent tension between art and science, and how resolutions to such tensions were carried forward into areas such the design semantics I briefly touched on in the previous chapter (it is of some interest that Klaus Krippendorff was a student at HfG Ulm). This historical backdrop provides some insight into why, e.g., Rune Monö states that "the product's message is formu-lated in a 'language' that we see, hear or feel. ... Within product semiotics, these signs consist of forms, colors, sounds and so on—in other words, elements that we usually associate with aesthetics" (Monö 1997, 21).

4. UbiComp, http://ubicomp.org (accessed October 21, 2016).

5. Our work also offers such examples of transitioning: the design research program Static! (2004–2005) came about after a pilot project (the Energy Curtain) and came to include a number of projects (or experiments, as we called them) before it ended (Mazé 2010). Later, core ideas of Static! evolved into a much larger research program by the Swedish Energy Agency (which also funded Static!) called "Energy, IT, and Design" (initiated in 2006 and still ongoing as of 2016), including open funding calls for research projects. Another example would be "IT + Textiles" (2001–2004) and its development from initial design experiments such as the Information Deliverer to the research program "Smart Textiles," led by the Swedish School of Textiles (Redström, Redström, and Mazé 2005).

6. Sometimes, however, such disagreements do get quite some attention—as in the case of a dress seemingly appearing as either white and gold or black and blue (e.g., "Is That Dress White and Gold or Blue and Black?" *New York Times*, February 27, 2015).

7. Consider the following example from Gilles Deleuze's reading of Henri Bergson:

Either we extract the abstract and general idea of color, and we do so by "effacing from red what makes it red, from blue what makes it blue, and from green what makes it green": then we are left with a concept which is a genre, and many objects for one concept. The concept and the object are two things, and the relation of the object to the concept is one of subsumption. Thus we get no farther than spatial distinctions, a state of difference that is external to the thing. Or we send the colors through a convergent lens that concentrates them on the same point: what we have then is "pure white light," the very light that "makes the differences come out between the shades." So, the different colors are no longer objects under a concept, but nuances or degrees of the concept itself. Degrees of difference itself, and not differences of degree. The relation is no longer one of subsumption, but one of participation. White light is still a universal, but a concrete universal, which gives us an understanding of the particular because it is the far end of the particular. (Deleuze 2004, 42)

Chapter 4

1. The centrality of "form" is also frequently reflected in names of organizations and publications, such as in *Die Form*, the periodical published by the Deutscher Werkbund; or Svensk Form, the Swedish Society of Crafts and Design.

2. The term "user" is also used in naming particular design domains, such as in designing "user interfaces" or "user experiences," or of certain methods such as "user testing," or in framing participation in a design process as "user involvement," and so on.

3. *Art Books 2008–Spring 2009* (Stockholm: Nationalmuseum), 17, http://www.nationalmuseum.se/Global/PDF/artbooks2008.pdf (accessed October 21, 2016).

4. The installation with the two chairs was in a way made in relation to Joseph Kosuth's conceptual art piece *One and Three Chairs* from 1965, in which a chair sits

alongside a photograph of a chair and a printed poster with a dictionary definition of the word "chair." If Kosuth's piece explored the issue of what a chair is, then the installation at the Nationalmuseum explored different acts of appreciating one—to look or to sit, to perceive something from a distance or to experience it through use—thus reflecting the context of what acts form the foundation for perceiving form at the museum.

5. In *Critique of Judgment*, Kant's account of aesthetic judgment and notions such as taste and beauty, he makes the following remark in the initial outline: "A judgment of taste, on the other hand, is merely contemplative, i.e., it is a judgment that is indifferent to the existence of the object: it [considers] the character of the object only by holding it up to our feeling of pleasure and displeasure. Nor is this contemplation, as such, directed to concepts, for a judgment of taste is not a cognitive judgment (whether theoretical or practical) and hence is neither based on concepts, nor directed to them as purposes" (Kant 1790, §5, p. 51).

6. Cf. Karen Barad's remark: "Performativity, properly construed, is not an invitation to turn everything (including material bodies) into words; on the contrary, performativity is precisely a contestation of the excessive power granted to language to determine what is real" (Barad 2007, 133).

7. For another illustration of the power of this way of relating to something, and the resilience of the two- or three-dimensional visual notion of form, consider an example from archeology. Asking the question "Why do archaeologists see architecture as perfect and complete instances of idea-objects, when their discipline is defined by its time-depth?" Lesley McFadyen provides an interesting illustration:

Archaeologists draw to better understand the things that are there in front of them, what it is they see, but in that process the drawing depicts more than the archaeologists' own designed intentions: it becomes the medium of an original design and so looks like the intentions of someone else. ... There is a real legacy here, and the plan has taken on an iconic status in archaeological accounts as if its graphic detail creates reality at a higher level of realism than the archaeological evidence itself. ... Perhaps more misleading, is that time is frozen, and every architectural feature exists at the same time on the surface of the page. ... Description has broken away from action and has become the explanation of something else. (McFadyen 2012, 105)

8. There are many other relevant examples from art and other areas. Consider, for instance, Nicolas Bourriaud's notion of "relational form":

We judge a work through its plastic or visual form. The most common criticism to do with new artistic practices consists, moreover, in denying them any "formal effectiveness," or in singling out their shortcomings in the "formal resolution." In observing contemporary artistic practices, we ought to talk of "formations" rather than "forms." Unlike an object that is closed in on itself by the intervention of a style and a signature, present-day art shows that form only exists in the encounter and in the dynamic relationship enjoyed by an artistic proposition with other formations, artistic or otherwise. ... What was yesterday regarded as formless or "informal" is no longer these things today. When the aesthetic discussion evolves, the status of form evolves along with it, and through it. (Bourriaud 2002, 21)

The kinds of work that Bourriaud refers to address not only a "new" kind of artistic expression but also explicitly the act of appreciating it—or, indeed, how the otherwise passive observer instead becomes part of the artwork, experimenting with the relation between spectator and participant, between form (or formation) and material.

9. John Cage's own account of *4′33″* offers a beautiful illustration of the difference between the two. In the following excerpt from a conversation, look to the difference between how he talks about the piece itself (as when talking about "the possibility of doing it," or that it would be "the highest form of work") and how he talks about its form and material (such as that it "opens you up to any possibility only when nothing is taken as the basis," and that it "has three movements and in all of the movements there are no sounds") (Kostelanetz 2003, 65):

Let me ask you a few questions about 4′33″. Is it true that it was actually conceived of in the late forties and just not presented until the fifties?

Yes. I knew about it, and had spoken about the possibility of doing it, for about four years before I did it.

Why were you hesitant?

I knew that it would be taken as a joke and a renunciation of work, whereas I also knew that if it was done it would be the highest form of work. Or this form of work: an art without work. I doubt whether many people understand it yet.

Well, the traditional understanding is that it opens you up to the sounds that exist around you and—

To the acceptance of anything, even when you have something as the basis. And that's how it's misunderstood.

What's a better understanding of it?

It opens you up to any possibility only when nothing is taken as the basis. But most people don't understand that, as far as I can tell. …

  I think perhaps my own best piece, at least the one I like the most, is the silent piece. … It has three movements and in all of the movements there are no sounds. I wanted my work to be free of my own likes and dislikes, because I think music should be free of the feelings and ideas of the composer. I have felt and hoped to have let other people to feel that the sounds of their environment constitute a music which is more interesting than the music which they would hear if they went into a concert hall.

  They missed the point. There's no such thing as silence. What they thought was silence [in *4′33″*], because they didn't know how to listen, was full of accidental sounds.

10. Indeed, basic principles are frequently introduced in studio-based teaching in this way, as in the following example from John Cage: "During a counterpoint class at UCLA, Schoenberg sent everybody to the blackboard. We were to solve a particular problem he had given and to turn around when finished so that he could check on the correctness of the solution. I did as directed. He said, 'That's good. Now find another solution.' I did. He said, 'Another.' Again I found one. Again he said, 'Another.' And so on. Finally, I said, 'There are no more solutions.' He said, 'What is the principle underlying all of the solutions?'" (Cage 1961, 93).

11. This has little or nothing to do with ideas such as "form follows function," and that proper form somehow emanates from a proper understanding of an object's functionality. Certainly the issue of form can be approached in that way, but what is at stake here is what we think form is: if form is what emerges to us as we look at a static object or image from a distance, or if we think of form as something more complex and variable.

And so one may think that a notion of form such as the one suggested here is completely at odds with historical ideas such as Kant's notion of disinterested contemplation, as I seem to replace the reflective appreciation from a distance so typical for most institutionalized ways of appreciating form with something more performative and akin to "experience in/of use." Certainly this would be a possibility, but this is not the primary purpose of the distinction, as it is also possible to stay close to such ideas about reflective contemplation.

Consider a road-racing bike, and "riding" as the act of appreciating its form (for examples, search bike reviews for remarks regarding a bike's "geometry"). Now think about the difference between using the bike to make the best possible time, and "riding" the bike with a focus on how it presents itself to you, how it feels, moves, sounds, etc. Clearly there is a difference between using the bike for competitive racing, and the act of riding as a basis for experiencing, reflecting on, and contemplating what it is, its form and materials. Or to use an example closer to existing institutionalized ways of appreciating form: could not performing a piece of music also be a matter of appreciating its form; would it not be strange to say that to appreciate musical form, you can only passively listen to it, not actively perform it? The difference between the two might be less radical than between racing with a bike and just looking at it, but there is still a difference between what comes forth from a distance and what emerges when performing, using, doing, making, etc., oneself.

Again, the primary distinction made with respect to form is not necessarily between whether the pleasure is disinterested or not, but rather what acts of appreciation we consider to be the ones privileged to define what form is.

12. "What Is Human-Centered Design?" IDEO.org, http://www.designkit.org/human-centered-design (accessed October 21, 2016).

Chapter 5

1. As is so often done in design and technology development, when the answer is already partly given in the question, the solution already pointed to in the problem: think of questions such as "How can we design information technology to improve the way we organize our meetings using online calendars?" or "How can we design everyday products to make people more aware of their energy consumption?" The only real difference between questions like these and an explicit assumption that design/technology can indeed do this, is the inclusion of a first "how," and the

order of the subsequent two words. The difference between "We can …!" and "How can we …?" is not very substantial, but we still seem to accept the latter as a legitimate form of "research question" in much design research.

2. See, e.g., Hallnäs and Redström 2006; Binder and Redström 2006; Brandt et al. 2011; Koskinen, Binder, and Redström 2008; Koskinen et al. 2011; Löwgren, Svarrer Larsen, and Hobye 2013.

3. United Nations Foundation, "What We Do: UN Agencies, Funds, and Programs," http://www.unfoundation.org/what-we-do/issues/united-nations/un-agencies-funds-and.html (accessed October 21, 2016).

4. CERN, "About CERN," https://home.cern/about (accessed October 21, 2016).

5. "Design" can refer to many different things, and different kinds of designing can be considered to have different kinds of foundations. In what follows, I focus on the kinds of ideas that govern many design schools, as well as the design histories written about areas such as industrial design, that is, design conceived as a kind of artistic practice. That said, I believe that similar stories can also be told about other kinds of designing stemming from scientific origins such as engineering.

6. As in the words of Harold Nelson and Erik Stolterman (2012, 41): "Design, as defined in this book, is different from other traditions of inquiry and action in that *service* is a defining element. Design is, by definition, a service relationship."

7. Kandinsky 1979; Paul Klee, *Bildnerische Form- Und Gestaltungslehre*, notebooks from Bauhaus teaching, 1921–1931, http://www.kleegestaltungslehre.zpk.org/ee/ZPK/Archiv/2011/01/25/00001 (accessed October 21, 2016).

8. Similar stories can also be told about design conducted in a scientific foundation, rather than an artistic one. Consider, for instance, addressing issues related to expressiveness in design engineering, as there is no real support for matters related to aesthetics and experience in the field's primary foundations in mathematics, physics, and the behavioral sciences. Also here will we find matters of great importance at the level of practice that have no real support in the original foundations of the discipline. For an informative illustration of how such differences need to be negotiated, see, e.g., Zimmerman, Forlizzi, and Evenson 2007.

9. Cf. the following remark by Stan Allen about the relation between practice and theory:

Today's conventional view (prevalent, for example, in schools of architecture) understands theory as an abstraction: a set of ideas and concepts independent of any particular material instance. Practice, in turn is understood as the *object* of theory. In this view, theory tends to envelope and protect practice, while practice excuses theory from the obligation to engage reality. Design is reduced to the implementation of rules set down elsewhere. Ironically, the separation that results is not dissimilar from the very structure of conventional practice supposedly challenged by theory. Conventional practice renounces theory, but in so doing, it simply reiterates unstated theoretical assumptions. … Theory imposes regulated ideological criteria over the undisciplined heterogeneity of the real, while the unstated assumptions of conventional practice enforce known solutions and safe repetitions. In both cases, small differences accumulate, but they never add up to make a difference. (Allen and Agrest 2000, xv–xvi)

10. Now, had this been a design program rather than a design *research* program, our decision to let it go for something else might well have turned out differently. A design program serving, say, the purpose of brand identity is not meant to be treated as inherently unstable—on the contrary, it is meant to be sustainable (if not static) over time. In that case, our interpretation of the program would have been different, and our interest much more oriented toward its optimal comfort zones than its breaking points. Thus here we also see one aspect of the difference between design set up for production and design set up for research.

11. Cf. Donna Haraway's remark on "situated knowledges": "I would like to insist on the embodied nature of all vision and so reclaim the sensory system that has been used to signify a leap out of the marked body and into a conquering gaze from nowhere. This is the gaze that mythically inscribes all the marked bodies, that makes the unmarked category claim the power to see and not be seen, to represent while escaping representation" (Haraway 1988, 581).

12. In some sense, this is related to the suspension of disbelief in fiction, and while some programs might be like science fiction, programs can just as well be about contemporary conditions. To illustrate, consider a program (or rather a programmatic design exercise) like the following:

To probe what "user-centered design" is, immediately replace the term "user" with a description of the very first image of a "user" that comes to your mind.

Say that your first image of a user is a white middle-class male. Will the difference between saying that one works with "user-centered design" and saying that one works with "white-middle-class-male-centered design" translate into an actual difference in design output? Will it *feel* different? Will others react differently when you explain what it is that you are doing? And what about encountering the work of others: what would be the difference between experiencing a thematic exhibition on "user-centered design" and one labeled "Scandinavian-middle-class-centered design" (and what if the exhibited objects as such were more or less the same in the two)?

The formulation of programs can also be a way to probe our worldviews, and what it is like to design as they bring otherwise not so visible basic beliefs to the forefront. And as discussed in the previous chapter, we use generic terms such as "users" to hide away all sorts of ideas and beliefs. For a related illustration, see the discussion that followed from Michael Burton and Michiko Nitta's "Republic of Salivation" (2010) as part of MoMA's "Design and Violence" project, http://designandviolence.moma.org/republic-of-salivation-michael-burton-and-michiko-nitta (accessed October 21, 2016); see also Antonelli and Hunt 2015; Prado and Oliveira 2014.

13. The three programmes—Lab, Field, and Showroom—discussed in Koskinen et al. 2011 are argued to be examples of large-scale programmatic structures that seemingly develop stability and scope over time. And while one might argue that they have value as foundations supporting design research development at the time when they came around, it will be interesting to see whether the stability they seem to gain over time will continue to support development, or if and when they will start to become degenerative.

14. One such example is the rewriting of the history of the discovery of the muon: "Two groups of workers detected the muon on the basis of cloud chamber studies of cosmic rays, together with the Bethe-Heitler energy-loss formula. History now has it that they were actually looking for Yukawa's 'meson,' and mistakenly thought they had found it—when in fact they had never heard of Yukawa's conjecture" (Hacking 1983, 161).

15. Indeed, this has been the case many times in my own work. Not only have we brought earlier experiments into a newly formulated program to *make sense* of it, but we have also frequently "reinterpreted" experiments from one program by bringing them with us into a new one. Especially in the very early and late stages of working with a program, certain experiments seem to even support such transitions. To give a concrete example: when working with the program Slow Technology (1999–2001) (Hallnäs and Redström 2001), our explorations of the materiality of computational technology led us in the direction of combining it with traditional materials in general, and over time with textiles in particular. This led to the formulation of a new research program called IT + Textiles (2001–2004) (Redström, Redström, and Mazé 2005), and one of the last experiments with slow technology, an "abstract information appliance" (Hallnäs and Redström 2002) called "an information deliverer" (Hallnäs, Melin, and Redström 2002), became one of the first experiments described as part of the IT + Textiles program. Later, another experiment, the "energy curtain," served a similar role in the transition from IT + Textiles to a program called Static (2004–2005) (Mazé 2010). See also Bang and Eriksen 2014; Brandt et al. 2011; Redström 2011.

16. Or, indeed, to move on to something quite different, such as commercial product development, without keeping much of its original programmatic connotations. A design made with the purpose of critical inquiry into issues of sustainability and consumption can, in spite of its origin, still be developed by someone else into yet another product for mass consumption.

17. E.g., http://www.merriam-webster.com/dictionary/stereotype (accessed October 21, 2016).

18. Indeed, as we explore notions of sameness rather than mere repetition, the repertoire of design examples created is likely to develop a "family resemblance," as discussed by Wittgenstein (1967).

Chapter 6

1. Other kinds of examples, of course, could be used for this, but a "problem" in design research with respect to more fundamental issues is the complete dominance of more compact forms for dissemination, such as papers and conference presentations. Such formats rarely offer space for more extensive exposure of all elements, as there is a need to focus on just a few key ideas, and it is therefore easy to simply avoid the more uneasy parts and their consequences.

2. Compare the following remark by Alex Seago and Anthony Dunne: "Like Michel Foucault's concept of a discourse which crosses and challenges traditional disciplinary territories, Dunne's research methodology does not readily fit into traditional analytical categories, because an attempt is being made to generate a different conception of the role of the design researcher/intellectual." Moreover, "In Dunne's case, the electronic object produced as the studio section of the doctorate is still 'design,' but in the sense of a 'material thesis' in which the object itself becomes a physical critique. ... Research is interpreted as 'conceptual modeling' involving a critique of existing approaches to production/consumption communicated through highly considered artifacts" (Seago and Dunne 1999, 16).

3. Compare the following remark by Erik Stolterman:

There is a need for studies on what kind of support interaction design practitioners actually care about and see as useful. ... Based on these and similar studies, it seems as if (interaction) design practitioners are inclined to appreciate and use: (i) precise and simple tools or techniques (sketching, prototypes, interviews, surveys, observations, etc.), (ii) frameworks that do not prescribe but that support reflection and decision-making (design patterns, ways of using prototypes, styles of interaction, etc.), (iii) individual concepts that are intriguing and open for interpretation and reflection on how they can be used (affordance, persona, probe, etc.), (iv) high-level theoretical and/or philosophical ideas and approaches that expand design thinking but do not prescribe design action (reflective practice, human-centered design, experience design, design rationale, etc.). (Stolterman 2008, 63)

4. Consider Donna Haraway's remark: "We need to learn in our bodies, endowed with primate color and stereoscopic vision, how to attach the objective to our theoretical and political scanners in order to name where we are and are not, in dimensions of mental and physical space we hardly know how to name. So, not so perversely, objectivity turns out to be about particular and specific embodiment and definitely not about the false vision promising transcendence of all limits and responsibility" (Haraway 1988, 582).

Chapter 7

1. Wittgenstein (1994):

6.54

My propositions serve as elucidations in the following way: anyone who understands me eventually recognizes them as nonsensical, when he has used them—as steps—to climb up beyond them. (He must, so to speak, throw away the ladder after he has climbed up it.)

He must transcend these propositions, and then he will see the world aright.

2. From a more philosophical point of view, there is something of an intellectual abyss next to this remark regarding what we talk about when we say "theory" and what is better articulated as a matter of "knowledge." I have tried my best to find my way around the edges of this abyss, the primary reason being that the issue of (forms of) knowledge already plays such a central role in much discourse on artistic and practice-based research (e.g., Borgdorff 2010). Working on the basis of notions such as ostensive definitions, I have instead tried to find another perspective that would allow me to point to structural and functional similarities and differences between the kind of design theory discussed here and what we typically consider theory to be like, since I believe it is crucial that we give such similarities and differences a critical look.

3. To further illustrate, in an interview by Sonali Shah, the windsurfing pioneer Larry Stanley describes how the addition of footstraps to the board "redefined" wavesailing in the late 1970s:

There was a new enthusiasm for jumping and we were all trying to outdo each other by jumping higher and higher. The problem was that … the riders flew off in mid-air because there was no way to keep the board with you—and as a result you hurt your feet, your legs, and the board.

Then I remembered the "Chip," a small experimental board we had built with footstraps, and thought "it's dumb not to use this for jumping." That's when I first started jumping with footstraps and discovering controlled flight. I could go so much faster than I ever thought and when you hit a wave it was like a motorcycle rider hitting a ramp; you just flew into the air. All of a sudden not only could you fly into the air, but you could land the thing, and not only that, but you could change direction in the air!

The whole sport of high-performance windsurfing really started from that. As soon as I did it, there were about ten of us who sailed all the time together and within one or two days there were various boards out there that had footstraps of various kinds on them, and we were all going fast and jumping waves and stuff. It just kind of snowballed from there. (von Hippel 2005, 1)

References

Aicher, Otl. 1991. Bauhaus and Ulm. In *Ulm Design: The Morality of Objects; Hochschule für Gestaltung Ulm, 1953–1968*, ed. Herbert Lindinger. Cambridge, MA: MIT Press.

Akrich, Madeleine. 1992. The De-scription of technical objects. In *Shaping Technology/Building Society: Studies in Sociotechnical Change*, ed. Wiebe E. Bijker and John Law. Cambridge, MA: MIT Press.

Albers, Anni. 1968. Oral history interview with Anni Albers, July 5, 1968. Archives of American Art. Smithsonian Institution.

Albers, Anni. 2000. *Anni Albers: Selected Writings on Design*. Ed. Brenda Danilowitz. Hanover: University Press of New England.

Alexander, Christopher. 1979. *The Timeless Way of Building*. New York: Oxford University Press.

Allen, Stan, and Diana Agrest. 2000. *Practice: Architecture, Technique, and Representation*. London: Routledge.

Antonelli, Paola, and Jamer Hunt. 2015. *Design and Violence*. New York: Museum of Modern Art.

Apple Computer Inc. 1992. *Macintosh Human Interface Guidelines*. Reading, MA: Addison-Wesley.

Aristotle. *De Anima—On the Soul*. Trans. J. A. Smith. http://classics.mit.edu/Aristotle/soul.html.

Attfield, Judy. 2000. *Wild Things: The Material Culture of Everyday Life*. Oxford: Berg.

Bajarin, Tim. 2013. How tablets have redefined the rules of personal computing. *Time*, December 2. http://techland.time.com/2013/12/02/how-tablets-have-redefined-the-rules-of-personal-computing.

Bang, Anne Louise, and Mette Agger Eriksen. 2014. Experiments all the way in programmatic design research. *Artifact* 3 (2): 4.1–4.14.

Bang, Anne Louise, Peter Krogh, Martin Ludvigsen, and Thomas Markussen. 2012. The role of hypothesis in constructive design research. In *Proceedings of the Art of Research Conference IV*. Helsinki: Aalto University School of Arts, Design and Architecture.

Barad, Karen Michelle. 2007. *Meeting the Universe Halfway: Quantum Physics and the Entanglement of Matter and Meaning*. Durham, NC: Duke University Press.

Bardzell, Jeffrey, and Shaowen Bardzell. 2013. What is critical about critical design? In *Proceedings of the SIGCHI Conference on Human Factors in Computing Systems*. New York: ACM.

Bergström, Greta, Carin Boalt, and Sten Lindgren. 1947. Kost och kök. 1. Stadsköket. In *HFI-Meddelanden, Årgång 2*, ed. Bo Gunnar Lindgren. Stockholm: Hemmens Forskningsinstitut.

Biggs, Michael, and Henrik Karlsson. 2010. Evaluating quality in artistic research. In *The Routledge Companion to Research in the Arts*, ed. Michael Biggs and Henrik Karlsson. London: Routledge.

Binder, Thomas, and Johan Redström. 2006. Exemplary design research. In *Proceedings of Wonderground, 2006 Design Research Society International Conference*. Lisbon: Design Research Society.

Borgdorff, Henk. 2010. The production of knowledge in artistic research. In *The Routledge Companion to Research in the Arts*, ed. Michael Biggs and Henrik Karlsson. London: Routledge.

Bourriaud, Nicolas. 2002. *Relational Aesthetics*. Trans. Mathieu Copeland, Fronza Woods, and Simon Pleasance. Dijon: Les Presses du Réel.

Brandt, Eva, Johan Redström, Mette Agger Eriksen, and Thomas Binder. 2011. *XLAB*. Copenhagen: Danish Design School Press.

Branzi, Andrea. 1984. *The Hot House: Italian New Wave Design*. Cambridge, MA: MIT Press.

Branzi, Andrea. 1988. *Learning from Milan: Design and the Second Modernity*. Trans. H. Evans. Cambridge, MA: MIT Press.

Bredies, Katharina. 2016. Introduction to *Design as Research*, ed. Gesche Joost, Katharina Bredies, Michelle Christensen, Florian Conradi, and Andreas Unteidig. Basel: Birkhäuser.

Bruns, C., H. Cottam, C. Vanstone, and J. Winhall. 2006. *Transformation Design*. RED paper 02. London: Design Council.

Buchanan, Richard. 1985. Declaration by design: Rhetoric, argument, and demonstration in design practice. *Design Issues* 2 (1): 4–22.

Cage, John. 1961. *Silence: Lectures and Writings*. Middletown, CT: Wesleyan University Press.

Carlgren, Gunilla, Gert Nyberg, and Brita Holme. 1947. Hushållsknivar. 1. Förskärare och rensknivar. In *HFI-Meddelanden, Årgång 2*, ed. Bo Gunnar Lindgren. Stockholm: Hemmens Forskningsinstitut.

Cooper, Rachel. 2016. Design research—no boundaries. In *Design as Research*, ed. Gesche Joost, Katharina Bredies, Michelle Christensen, Florian Conradi, and Andreas Unteidig. Basel: Birkhäuser.

Cross, Nigel. 2001. Designerly ways of knowing: Design discipline versus design science. *Design Issues* 17 (3): 49–55.

Debord, Guy. 1983. *Society of the Spectacle*. Detroit: Black & Red.

de Certeau, Michel. 1984. *The Practice of Everyday Life*. Berkeley: University of California Press.

Deleuze, Gilles. 1995. *Negotiations, 1972–1990*. New York: Columbia University Press.

Deleuze, Gilles. 2004. *Desert Islands and Other Texts, 1953–1974*. Los Angeles: Semiotext(e).

Deleuze, Gilles, and Félix Guattari. 1994. *What Is Philosophy?* New York: Columbia University Press.

Design Council. 2007. *A Study of the Design Process*. London: Design Council. http://www.designcouncil.org.uk/sites/default/files/asset/document/ElevenLessons_Design_Council%20(2).pdf.

Dilnot, Clive. 2015. History, design, futures: Contending with what we have made. In *Design and the Question of History*, ed. Tony Fry, Clive Dilnot, and Susan C. Stewart. London: Bloomsbury.

Djajadiningrat, Tom, Kees Overbeeke, and Stephan Wensveen. 2002. But how, Donald, tell us how? On the creation of meaning in interaction design through feedforward and inherent feedback. In *Proceedings of the 4th Conference on Designing Interactive Systems: Processes, Practices, Methods, and Techniques*. New York: ACM.

Dourish, Paul. 2001. *Where the Action Is: The Foundations of Embodied Interaction*. Cambridge, MA: MIT Press.

Dunin-Woyseth, Halina, and Fredrik Nilsson. 2013. Emerging "doctorateness" in creative fields of architecture, art and design. In *Artistic Research Then and Now: 2004–2013*, ed. Torbjörn Lind. Stockholm: Swedish Research Council.

Dunne, Anthony. 1999. *Hertzian Tales: Electronic Products, Aesthetic Experience and Critical Design*. London: RCA CRD Research Publications.

Dunne, Anthony, and Fiona Raby. 2001. *Design Noir: The Secret Life of Electronic Objects*. Basel: Birkhäuser.

Dunne, Anthony, and Fiona Raby. 2013. *Speculative Everything: Design, Fiction, and Social Dreaming*. Cambridge, MA: MIT Press.

Ehn, Pelle. 1989. *Work-Oriented Design of Computer Artifacts*. Stockholm: Arbetslivcentrum.

Ericsson, Magnus, and Ramia Mazé, eds. 2011. *Design Act: Socially and Politically Engaged Design Today—Critical Roles and Emerging Tactics*. Stockholm: IASPIS and Sternberg Press.

Foucault, Michel. 1977. *Discipline and Punish: The Birth of the Prison*. Trans. A. Sheridan. New York: Vintage.

Frayling, Christopher. 1993. Research in art and design. *Royal College of Art Research Papers* 1 (1): 1–5.

Friedman, Ken. 2003. Theory construction in design research: Criteria; Approaches, and methods. *Design Studies* 24 (6): 507–522.

Fry, Tony. 2009. *Design Futuring: Sustainability, Ethics, and New Practice*. Oxford: Berg.

Gaver, William. 2012. What should we expect from research through design? In *Proceedings of the SIGCHI Conference on Human Factors in Computing Systems*. New York: ACM.

Gropius, Walter. 1970. Principles of Bauhaus production. In *Programs and Manifestoes on 20th-Century Architecture*, ed. Ulrich Conrads. Cambridge, MA: MIT Press. Originally published in 1926.

Hacking, Ian. 1983. *Representing and Intervening: Introductory Topics in the Philosophy of Natural Science*. Cambridge: Cambridge University Press.

Hackos, JoAnn T., and Janice Redish. 1998. *User and Task Analysis for Interface Design*. New York: Wiley.

Hall, Ashley. 2011. Experimental design: Design experimentation. *Design Issues* 27 (2): 17–26.

Hallnäs, Lars. 2010. The design research text and the poetics of foundational definitions. *Art Monitor* 2010 (8). http://hdl.handle.net/2077/24659.

Hallnäs, Lars, Linda Melin, and Johan Redström. 2002. Textile displays: Using textiles to investigate computational technology as design material. In *Proceedings of the Second Nordic Conference on Human-Computer Interaction*. New York: ACM.

Hallnäs, Lars, and Johan Redström. 2001. Slow technology—designing for reflection. *Personal and Ubiquitous Computing* 5 (3): 201–212.

Hallnäs, Lars, and Johan Redström. 2002. Abstract information appliances: Methodological exercises in conceptual design of computational things. In *Proceedings of the 4th Conference on Designing Interactive Systems: Processes, Practices, Methods, and Techniques*. New York: ACM.

Hallnäs, Lars, and Johan Redström. 2006. *Interaction Design: Foundations, Experiments*. Borås: Interactive Institute and Textile Research Centre, Swedish School of Textiles, University College of Borås.

Hamilton, Richard. 1960. Persuading image. *Design* 134:28–32.

Hancock, T., and C. Bezold. 1994. Possible futures, preferable futures. *Health Forum Journal* 37 (2): 23–29.

Haraway, Donna. 1988. Situated knowledges: The science question in feminism and the privilege of partial perspective. *Feminist Studies* 14 (3): 575–599.

Heidegger, Martin. 2008. The question concerning technology. In *Basic Writings: From Being and Time (1927) to The Task of Thinking (1964)*, trans. D. F. Krell. New York: Harper Perennial Modern Thought.

Hemmens Forskningsinstitut. 1946. *HFI-Meddelanden Nr 1: Diskning*. Ed. Bo Gunnar Lindgren. Stockholm.

Henchey, Norman. 1978. Making sense of future studies. *Alternatives* 7:24–29.

Hensel, Michael U. and Fredrik Nilsson. 2016. Introduction to *The Changing Shape of Practice: Integrating Research and Design in Architecture*, ed. Michael U. Hensel and Fredrik Nilsson. New York: Routledge.

Hickey, Amber, Angelina Köpplin, and Mary Tremonte. 2012. *A Guidebook of Alternative Nows*. Los Angeles: Journal of Aesthetics and Protest Press.

Hill, Jonathan. 1998. An other architect. In *Occupying Architecture: Between the Architect and the User*, ed. Jonathan Hill. London: Routledge.

Höök, Kristina, and Jonas Löwgren. 2012. Strong concepts: Intermediate-level knowledge in interaction design research. *ACM Transactions on Computer-Human Interaction* 19 (3): 23.

Houde, Stephanie, and Charles Hill. 1997. What do prototypes prototype? In *Handbook of Human-Computer Interaction*, 2nd ed., ed. Martin Helander, Thomas Landauer, and Prasad Prabhu. Amsterdam: Elsevier.

Hunt, Jamer. 2003. Just re-do it: Tactical formlessness and everyday consumption. In *Strangely Familiar: Design and Everyday Life*, ed. Andrew Blauvelt. Minneapolis: Walker Art Center.

Ihde, Don. 1993. *Philosophy of Technology: An Introduction*. New York: Paragon House.

Jones, John Chris. 1984. *Essays in Design*. New York: Wiley.

Jones, John Chris. 1988. Softecnica. In *Design after Modernism: Beyond the Object*, ed. John Thackara. New York: Thames & Hudson.

Jones, John Chris. 1992. *Design Methods*. 2nd edition. New York: Van Nostrand Reinhold.

Joost, Gesche, Katharina Bredies, Michelle Christensen, Florian Conradi, and Andreas Unteidig, eds. 2016. *Design as Research*. Basel: Birkhäuser.

Kandinsky, Wassily. 1979. *Point and Line to Plane*. Trans. H. Dearstyne and H. Rebay. New York: Dover.

Kant, Immanuel. (1790) 1987. *Critique of Judgment*. Trans. Werner S. Pluhar. Indianapolis: Hackett.

Karlsson, Monica Lindh, and Johan Redström. 2015. Design togetherness. In *Design Ecologies: Proceedings of the Nordic Design Research Conference 2015* . Stockholm: Nordes..

Karlsson, Monica Lindh, and Johan Redström. 2016. Design togetherness, pluralism and convergence. In *Proceedings of DRS 2016, Design Research Society 50th Anniversary Conference*. Brighton: Design Research Society.

Kepes, György. 1969. Education of the eye. In *The Bauhaus: Weimar, Dessau, Berlin, Chicago*, ed. Hans Maria Wingler. Cambridge, MA: MIT Press.

Kepes, György. 1995. *Language of Vision*. New York: Dover.

Koskinen, Ilpo, Thomas Binder, and Johan Redström. 2008. Lab, field, gallery, and beyond. *Artifact* 2 (1): 46–57.

Koskinen, Ilpo, John Zimmerman, Thomas Binder, Johan Redström, and Stephan Wensveen. 2011. *Design Research through Practice: From the Lab, Field, and Showroom*. Waltham, MA: Morgan Kaufmann/Elsevier.

Kossoff, Gideon, Terry Irwin, and Anne-Marie Willis. 2016. Transition design. Special issue, *Design Philosophy Papers* 13 (1).

Kostelanetz, Richard. 2003. *Conversing with Cage*. New York: Routledge.

Krippendorff, Klaus. 2016. Design, an undisciplinable profession. In *Design as Research*, ed. Gesche Joost, Katharina Bredies, Michelle Christensen, Florian Conradi, and Andreas Unteidig. Basel: Birkhäuser.

Krippendorff, Klaus, and Reinhart Butter. 1984. Product semantics: Exploring the symbolic qualities of form. *Innovation* 3 (2): 4.

Kwinter, Sanford. 1994. Who's afraid of formalism? *Any Magazine* 7–8:65.

Lakatos, Imre, and Paul Feyerabend. 1999. *For and Against Method: Including Lakatos's Lectures on Scientific Method and the Lakatos-Feyerabend Correspondence*. Ed. Matteo Motterlini. Chicago: University of Chicago Press.

Latour, Bruno. 2010. An attempt at a "compositionist manifesto." *New Literary History* 41 (3): 471–490.

Löwgren, Jonas. 2007. Inspirational patterns for embodied interaction. *Knowledge, Technology, and Policy* 20 (3): 165–177.

Löwgren, Jonas, Henrik Svarrer Larsen, and Mads Hobye. 2013. Towards programmatic design research. *Designs for Learning* 6 (1–2): 80–100.

Mäkelä, Maarit. 2006. Framing (a) practice-led research project. In *The Art of Research: Research Practices in Art and Design*, ed. Maarit Mäkelä and Sara Routarinne. Helsinki: University of Art and Design Helsinki.

Maldonado, Tomás. 1991. Looking back at Ulm. In *Ulm Design: The Morality of Objects; Hochschule für Gestaltung Ulm, 1953–1968*, ed. Herbert Lindinger. Cambridge, MA: MIT Press.

Mazé, Ramia, ed. 2010. *Static! Designing for Energy Awareness*. Stockholm: Arvinius.

Mazé, Ramia, Judith Gregory, and Johan Redström. 2011. Social sustainability: A design research approach to sustainable development. In *Proceedings of the 4th World Conference on Design Research (IASDR)*. Delft, Netherlands: IASDR.

McFadyen, Lesley. 2012. The time it takes to make: Design and use in architecture and archaeology. In *Design and Anthropology*, ed. Wendy Gunn and Jared Donovan. Farnham: Ashgate.

Merleau-Ponty, Maurice. 1968. The intertwining—the chiasm. In *The Visible and the Invisible*, ed. Claude Lefort, trans. Alphonso Lingis. Evanston: Northwestern University Press.

Mitchell, C. Thomas. 1993. *Redefining Designing: From Form to Experience*. New York: Van Nostrand Reinhold.

Mitchell, C. 2002. *User-Responsive Design: Reducing the Risk of Failure*. New York: Norton.

Moggridge, Bill. 2007. *Designing Interactions*. Cambridge, MA: MIT Press.

Moholy-Nagy, László. 1998. The new typography. In *Modernism: An Anthology of Sources and Documents*, ed. Vassiliki Kolocotroni, Jane Goldman, and Olga Taxidou. Edinburgh: Edinburgh University Press. Originally published in 1923.

Moholy-Nagy, Sibyl. 1950. *Moholy-Nagy: Experiment in Totality*. New York: Harper.

Monö, Rune. 1997. *Design for Product Understanding: The Aesthetics of Design from a Semiotic Approach*. Trans. M. Knight. Stockholm: Liber.

Nelson, Harold G., and Erik Stolterman. 2012. *The Design Way: Intentional Change in an Unpredictable World*. Cambridge, MA: MIT Press.

Nietzsche, Friedrich. 1968. *The Will to Power*. Trans. W. Kaufmann and R. J. Hollingdale. New York: Random House.

Nightingale, Andrea Wilson. 2001. On wandering and wondering: "Theôria" in Greek philosophy and culture. *Arion: A Journal of Humanities and the Classics* 9 (2): 23–58.

Overbeeke, Kees, Stephan Wensveen, and Caroline Hummels. 2006. Design research: Generating knowledge through doing. In *Proceedings of the 3rd Symposium of Design Research: Drawing New Territories*. Geneva: Swiss Design Network.

Parsons, Tim. 2009. *Thinking: Objects; Contemporary Approaches to Product Design*. Lausanne: AVA Publishing.

Pierce, James, Phoebe Sengers, Tad Hirsch, Tom Jenkins, William Gaver, and Carl DiSalvo. 2015. Expanding and refining design and criticality in HCI. In *Proceedings of the 33rd Annual ACM Conference on Human Factors in Computing Systems*. New York: ACM.

Pierce, James, Yolande Strengers, Phoebe Sengers, and Susanne Bødker, eds. 2013. Special issue on practice-oriented approaches to sustainable HCI. *ACM Transactions on Computer-Human Interaction* 20 (4).

Prado, Luiza, and Pedro Oliveira. 2014. Questioning the critical in speculative and critical design. *Medium*. https://medium.com/a-parede/questioning-the-critical-in-speculative-critical-design-5a355cac2ca4#.ifazzw842.

Preece, Jenny, Yvonne Rogers, and Helen Sharp. 2002. *Interaction Design: Beyond Human-Computer Interaction*. New York: J. Wiley & Sons.

Pullen, John Patrick. 2015. Will Angela Ahrendts redefine luxury with the launch of the new Apple Watch? *Fortune*, March 11. http://fortune.com/2015/03/11/angela-ahrendts.

RAE2008. 2006. RAE2008, Research Assessment Exercise, Panel criteria and working methods, Panel O, UOA 63: Art and Design. http://www.rae.ac.uk/panels/main/o/art/.

Redström, Johan. 2001. Designing everyday computational things. PhD thesis, Gothenburg Studies in Informatics, no. 20.

Redström, Johan. 2006a. Persuasive design: Fringes and foundations. In *Persuasive Technology*, ed. Wijnand A. IJsselsteijn, Yvonne A. W. de Kort, Cees Midden, Berry Eggen, and Elise van den Hoven. Berlin: Springer.

Redström, Johan. 2006b. Towards user design? On the shift from object to user as the subject of design. *Design Studies* 27 (2): 123–139.

Redström, Johan. 2008. RE: Definitions of use. *Design Studies* 29 (4): 410–423.

Redström, Johan. 2011. Some notes on programme-experiment dialectics. In *Nordes 2011: Nordic Design Research Conference*. Helsinki: Nordes.

Redström, Johan. 2012. Defining moments. In *Design and Anthropology*, ed. Wendy Gunn and Jared Donovan. Farnham: Ashgate.

Redström, Johan. 2013. Form-Acts: A critique of conceptual cores. In *Share This Book: Critical Perspectives and Dialogues about Design and Sustainability*, ed. Ramia Mazé, Lisa Olausson, Matilda Plöjel, Johan Redström, and Christina Zetterlund. Stockholm: Axl Books.

Redström, Maria, Johan Redström, and Ramia Mazé, eds. 2005. *IT + Textiles*. Helsinki: Edita/IT Press.

Rittel, Horst W. J. 1991. The HfG legacy? In *Ulm Design: The Morality of Objects; Hochschule für Gestaltung Ulm, 1953–1968*, ed. Herbert Lindinger. Cambridge, MA: MIT Press.

Russell, Bertrand. 1948. *Human Knowledge: Its Scope and Limits*. New York: Simon & Schuster.

Schatzki, Theodore R. 2001a. Introduction to *The Practice Turn in Contemporary Theory*, ed. Theodore R. Schatzki, Eike von Savigny, and Karin Knorr-Cetina. London: Routledge.

Schatzki, Theodore R. 2001b. Practice mind-ed orders. In *The Practice Turn in Contemporary Theory*, ed. Theodore R. Schatzki, Eike von Savigny, and Karin Knorr-Cetina. London: Routledge.

Schön, Donald A. 1983/1991. *The Reflective Practitioner: How Professionals Think in Action*. Aldershot: Ashgate.

Seago, Alex, and Anthony Dunne. 1999. New methodologies in art and design research: The object as discourse. *Design Issues* 15 (2): 11–17.

Sheldon, Roy, and Arens Egmont. 1932. *Consumer Engineering: A New Technique for Prosperity*. New York: Harper.

Shove, Elizabeth, Matthew Watson, Martin Hand, and Jack Ingram. 2007. *The Design of Everyday Life*. Oxford: Berg.

Simon, Herbert A. 1996. *The Sciences of the Artificial*. Cambridge, MA: MIT Press.

Smets, Gerda, and Kees Overbeeke. 1994. Industrial design engineering and the theory of direct perception. *Design Studies* 15 (2): 175–184.

Stappers, Pieter Jan. 2007. Doing design as a part of doing research. In *Design Research Now: Essays and Selected Projects*, ed. Ralf Michel. Basel: Birkhäuser.

Steffen, Dagmar. 2014. New experimentalism in design research: Characteristics and interferences of experiments in science, the arts and in design research. *Artifact* 3 (2): 1.1–1.16.

Stolterman, Erik. 2008. The nature of design practice and implications for interaction design research. *International Journal of Design* 2 (1): 55–65.

Telier, A., Thomas Binder, Giorgio De Michelis, Pelle Ehn, Giulio Jacucci, Per Linde, and Ina Wagner. 2011. *Design Things*. Cambridge, MA: MIT Press.

Tonkinwise, Cameron. 2005. Is design finished? Dematerialisation and changing things. *Design Philosophy Papers* 3 (2): 99–117.

Tonkinwise, Cameron. 2014. Design studies: What is it good for? *Design and Culture* 6 (1): 5–43.

Tschumi, Bernard. 1996. *Architecture and Disjunction*. Cambridge, MA: MIT Press.

von Hippel, Eric. 2005. *Democratizing Innovation*. Cambridge, MA: MIT Press.

Voros, Joseph. 2003. A generic foresight process framework. *Foresight* 5 (3): 10–21.

Weiser, Mark. 1991. The computer for the 21st century. *Scientific American* 265 (3): 94–104.

Weiser, Mark. 1993. Some computer science issues in ubiquitous computing. *Communications of the ACM* 36 (7): 75–84.

Weiser, Mark. 1996. The testbed devices of the infrastructure for ubiquitous computing project. http://www.ubiq.com/weiser/testbeddevices.htm.

Winnicott, Donald Woods. 1953. Transitional objects and transitional phenomena. *International Journal of Psychoanalysis* 34:89.

Wittgenstein, Ludwig. 1967. *Philosophische Untersuchungen. Philosophical Investigations*. Trans. G. E. M. Anscombe. Reprinted. Blackwell.

Wittgenstein, Ludwig. 1994. *Tractatus Logico-Philosophicus*. Trans. D. Pears and B. McGuiness. London: Routledge.

Zetterlund, Christina. 2013. Beyond institutionalized practice: Exhibition as a way of understanding craft and design. In *Share This Book: Critical Perspectives and Dialogues about Design and Sustainability*, ed. Ramia Mazé, Lisa Olausson, Matilda Plöjel, Johan Redström, and Christina Zetterlund. Stockholm: Axl Books.

Zetterlund, Christina, and Matilda Plöjel, eds. 2008. *Undersöka form*. Vols. 1–3. Stockholm: Nationalmuseum.

Zimmerman, John, Jodi Forlizzi, and Shelley Evenson. 2007. Research through design as a method for interaction design research in HCI. In *Proceedings of the SIGCHI Conference on Human Factors in Computing Systems*. New York: ACM.

Index

Page numbers followed by an "f" indicate figures.